The Crimson Path

The Foreshadows and Fulfillment of the Lamb of God!

ROBERT D. FINLEY

WESTBOW
PRESS®
A DIVISION OF THOMAS NELSON
& ZONDERVAN

WestBow Press books may be ordered through booksellers or by contacting:

WestBow Press
A Division of Thomas Nelson & Zondervan
1663 Liberty Drive
Bloomington, IN 47403
www.westbowpress.com
1 (866) 928-1240

Because of the dynamic nature of the Internet, any web addresses or links contained in this book may have changed since publication and may no longer be valid. The views expressed in this work are solely those of the author and do not necessarily reflect the views of the publisher, and the publisher hereby disclaims any responsibility for them.

Any people depicted in stock imagery provided by Thinkstock are models, and such images are being used for illustrative purposes only. Certain stock imagery © Thinkstock.

ISBN: 978-1-5127-3382-2 (sc)
ISBN: 978-1-5127-3383-9 (hc)
ISBN: 978-1-5127-3381-5 (e)

Library of Congress Control Number: 2016903715

Print information available on the last page.

WestBow Press rev. date: 03/08/2016

Robert Finley has provided a very insightful resource for the Christian church; thorough, encouraging, and will help every reader understand the biblical teaching that Jesus Christ is the Lamb of God.

Dr. Brad Jurkovich
Pastor of First Baptist Church
Bossier City, Louisiana

Dr. Robert Finley has done a grand work in writing about the blood. You will benefit greatly from this tracing of the blood that takes away our sin. In a culture (even in religious circles) that prides itself with no absolute truth, it is a blessing indeed to learn from Genesis to Revelation that the precious blood of Jesus is always relevant. Thank you, Bro. Robert for an excellent work.

Dr. Bill Elton
Pastor First Baptist Church
Fountain Hill, Arkansas

Dr. Robert Finley is an incredible man of God, and his book, "The Crimson Path: the Foreshadows and Fulfillment of the Lamb of God" is not only timely, but extremely accurate! He has taken great detail and gone into in-depth study to present a work that laymen, Bible teachers and pastors can rely on for years! I count it a privilege to have him as one of our resident theologians here in our church, but also to call him a friend.

Frank Teat
Pastor of Connections
First Baptist Church
Bossier City, Louisiana

DEDICATION

This work is dedicated to my Lady and wife, Nell. Throughout this endeavor, she was my strongest supporter, daily encourager, and chief editor. Nell endured countless hours as a 'school widow' while I completed the required course work. My heart remains full of thanksgiving to my Lord for her immeasurable assistance, her determination to keep me motivated, and for her unwavering love. My sincerest thanks for walking this journey with me. I love you.

Contents

INTRODUCTION

Have you ever wondered why John the Baptist introduced Jesus Christ to Israel as the 'Lamb of God' in John 1:29? Israel eagerly anticipated the arrival of their Messiah. They longed for His deliverance! Yet, they refused to receive Jesus Christ as their prophesied Messiah. It seems there were numerous other titles with which John the Baptist could have addressed Jesus; titles that would have invoked an immediate acceptance of Jesus as the 'Christ', or Messiah. Why not introduce Him as the promised heir to the throne of King David? The Jewish populace was anxiously awaiting their Messiah to come as a militant deliverer—a mighty lion; not a humble Lamb. Yet, John the Baptist first proclaimed Jesus as the 'Lamb of God' and later testified of Him as the 'Son of God'. John went straight to the heart and need of Israel and the entire world. All needed "The Lamb of God who taketh away the sin of the world!"

A foreshadow is a person, event, ritual, or thing, that represents, indicates, or typifies something beforehand. It implies a certain dimness, but also suggests some resemblance between two things.[1] This exposition will examine 'foreshadows' of a coming event that will culminate in the fulfillment of, or completion of, a plan devised by God Almighty Himself. This plan would forever change the world and the lives of those who, in faith, would embrace His plan.

The following pages will take the reader on a journey, a journey through the ages. Along this journey, together we will discover each

---

[1] Jerry Allen. *The Scarlet Cord, Foreshadows of Christ-a Mystery Revealed* (Seattle, Washington: Booksurge Publishing, 2009) 18.

foreshadow revealed in the pages of a sacred inspired book, the Bible. We will seek to see and understand the resemblance of the event recorded and correlate it with the plan of fulfillment. As the Bible states, "But when the fulness of the time was come, God sent forth his Son, made of a woman, made under the law, to redeem them that were under the law, that we might receive the adoption of sons" (Galatians 4:4-5).

As on any lengthy journey, stops will be made along the way. Each stop will acquaint one with a foreshadow of God's ultimate fulfillment. An assessment will be made of the characters, the setting, and sequence of each event, as well as the role they portray in each foreshadow. This journey will take one to a hill outside of Jerusalem called Calvary, the place of a skull. It was on this hill the 'Lamb of God', man's Savior, made the ultimate sacrifice for the redemption of man.

The path embarked upon will begin in the Old Testament to enable one to understand who this Savior was and what He did. Each foreshadow given provides a glimpse of the redemptive work of this Savior. Each foreshadow will be examined as an individual piece of a puzzle, or a piece of 'the mystery of the gospel' (Ephesians 6:19). Hopefully, as the puzzle, or 'mystery', is completed and the gracious plan of God unfolds, each glimpse or portrayal of the sacrifice will provide illumination. The journey begins in the book of Genesis.

In the beginning, after turning darkness into light, dividing the waters to create dry land, covering the land with vegetation, hanging the sun, moon, and the stars, creating the creatures of the sea, air, and land, God crowned the spectacular creation of all His awesome wonders with the creation of Man, Adam. God's intended purpose was to have intimate fellowship with man in His sinless world. God placed Adam in a place of utopia called Eden. The Creator came daily to this place of perfection to commune with His beloved creation. Man's attribute of innocence allowed fellowship between him and Holy God.

Before the foundations of the world, God, in His infinite knowledge, knew man would sin. God looked through the portals of time and saw mankind's greatest need. He would need a way back to God! Man would need a Savior! One fateful day, God came for his daily communion and discovered Adam hiding, for he feared to face his

Creator. Adam's fear stemmed from his willful disobedience, sin, against Holy God. Though Adam made a futile attempt to cover his guilt, all-knowing God confronted Adam and brought him to acknowledge his sin. Consequences of disobedience had been pre-disclosed; therefore, judgment and justice had to be rendered. Judgment was death: spiritual and physical.

Man's inability to satisfy God's righteousness and avoid His wrath resulted in God's intervention on man's behalf. Man's feeble attempt to cover his shame resulted in the unfolding of God's redemptive plan. God's requirement for the atonement of sin necessitated a blood sacrifice. Man, unable to assuage his sin and reconcile himself unto God, was without hope. An innocent substitute was the only acceptable payment. The first animal was killed, the blood was shed, and the sins were forgiven. As demonstrated in the Garden of Eden, a precedent was established by the shedding of innocent blood to atone sin.

As God's redemptive road is traveled, the fluid continuity of the Old and New Testaments of Scripture will be discovered. Throughout the Old Testament Scriptures, God reveals silhouettes of His plan of atonement. Each silhouette is a portrayal of the ultimate sacrifice needed to forever cleanse man of his transgression. In the New Testament, the needed Savior came and shed His innocent blood to atone for man's sin, once and for all. This final act was the fulfillment of God's redemptive plan.

Although the works of many scholars have been consulted for this study, the primary source of reference is God's Holy word, the Bible. It is the belief of this writer that the Bible is the inspired, infallible, plenary, word of Holy God. The Bible is the final source of authority! It is important to note that within the pages of Scripture, God provides the reader with a progressive revelation of His plan. For example, Noah did not have as much enlightenment as Moses; Moses did not have the understanding that the prophet Isaiah had; Isaiah received only a shadow of knowledge compared to the New Testament disciples of Jesus, etc. It is within the Scriptures, God systematically unfolds His divine plan of atonement.

From the beginning of Genesis to the end of Revelation, the central theme is the redemptive work of the 'Lamb of God'. Jesus Christ is the *Alpha*, the beginning or first, and the *Omega*, the ending or the last. Jesus Christ is the crimson path which connects the Old and New Testaments.

Embark with me on a quest as we journey through the pages of the Old Testament and view the foreshadows of a divine plan devised by Almighty God. The journey will continue into the pages of the New Testament where the fulfillment of the plan of redemption is illuminated by the spilling of the blood of the Lamb. Behold, the Lamb of God! Worthy is the Lamb!

CHAPTER ONE

Alpha Lamb

With the roadmap, the Bible, in hand, let's begin the journey. As with all journeys, this journey, too, must begin at the beginning: Genesis One. The word, Genesis, means 'beginning'. Within the pages of Genesis, one discovers the beginning of all things as they are known. One is immediately introduced to the main character and the Author of all things, God Almighty: God, the One who had no beginning. He was before all things and shall have no end, God will always be! Very quickly within the narrative, one learns of the incomprehensible power of God. He *spoke* and a massive void of darkness became brilliant galaxies, filled with planets and glistening with a multitude of stars. "By the word of the LORD were the heavens made; and all the host of them by the breath of his mouth" (Psalm 33:6). Nothing became something; a spectacular creation came into existence!

When God created the heavens and earth, He created it in a mature state. The heavens were glittered with stars immediately twinkling; the sun rose in the east in its brilliance and set in the west in spectacular color. The moon rose on cue and offered its reflective glory each night. On earth, the marine life swam the clear currents, animal life grazed and frolicked along the uncluttered landscape, and the fowl of the air soared in the unpolluted sky. Full grown trees produced shade and shelter and fruit trees were loaded with their varieties of unspoiled fruit. No weeds intermingled with the lush grasses to blemish the beautiful landscape.

There was no blight to attack the earth's foliage. Roses blossomed without thorns, offering the sweetest fragrance. Vegetation produced the most bountiful and delicious nourishment. Though everything was newly created, there was the semblance of age.

There were no dark storm clouds awaiting to cover the pristine blue sky. No violent earthquakes rumbled beneath the earth's surface, awaiting to rearrange the topography. No volcanoes boiled in the earth's core, awaiting to spew destructive hot lava over the Creator's masterpiece. There was no drought to create barren space. No hurricanes were brewing in the vast oceans, awaiting to flood God's perfect creation.

Seas separated the land masses. Rivers flowed with crystal clear water. Majestic mountains towered above fertile valleys. The finger of God formed the river beds and canyons; not millions of years of erosion, contrary to the beliefs of geologists. "When I consider thy heavens, the work of thy fingers, the moon and the stars, which thou hast ordained" (Psalm 8:3). There has never been a more perfect environment; an environment totally unblemished by evil.

In the midst of this perfect environment, there was a place the Scriptures identify as Eden. The name Eden means 'delight' and what a delightful place it must have been. Eden has also been referred to as Paradise. Located on the eastern side of this beautiful and serene habitat, God planted a garden. This garden flourished with mature fruit bearing trees, which provided food and nourishment. Out of Eden flowed a river which watered the garden of God. In the midst of Eden could be found two very special and unique trees: the tree of life and the tree of knowledge of good and evil.

According to the notes found in the Liberty Annotated Study Bible, "these were two literal trees to which God gave some special significance."[2] There is not much revealed concerning these two trees, but emphasis is placed upon their significance and importance. One scholar wrote, "Thus "the tree of life" symbolizes opportunity to

---

[2] Jerry Falwell, ex. ed., *Liberty Annotated Study Bible* (Lynchburg, Virginia: Liberty University, 1988) 10, notes on Genesis 2:9.

experience the fulness of life as a fruitage of dominion over creation."[3] Further reference to the 'tree of life' is made in Revelation 2:7 and 22:2, 14. In Revelation 2:7, access to the tree of life will be given to all true Christians to eat from its fruit. This verse also places the location of the tree of life in the midst of the paradise of God. The references in Revelation 22:2 and 14, reveal that within the New Jerusalem, the tree of life is located on either side of the river which flowed from the throne of God and the Lamb. This tree will bear twelve manner of fruits and bear fruit each month. Interestingly, the Scriptures describe the leaves of the tree are for the healing of the nations. The inhabitants of the New Jerusalem will be given the right to access the tree of life and enter through the gates of the city. It appears, according to Scripture, the tree of life holds a significant role in the Christian experiencing fullness of life and continuous blessing.

The tree of knowledge of good and evil is mentioned only in Genesis 2:9, 17. In Hebrew the word used for 'knowledge' refers to experiential knowledge. The essence of the tree would be to "give men the power to decide for themselves what was in their best interest and what was not, and to be like God ... it would provide one with the experiential knowledge in good and evil; but it did not give one the strength to choose the good and reject the evil."[4] The beauty of this garden was unexcelled and unparalleled. It was in this complete and perfect environment that God placed the crown of His creation, man.

Man stood unique in the midst of all of God's glorious creation. "And out of the ground the LORD God formed every beast of the field, and every fowl of the air ..." (Genesis 2:19). "And the LORD God formed man of the dust of the ground, and breathed into his nostrils the breath of life; and man became a living soul" (Genesis 2:7). "Science has proven that every chemical element found in the body of man is

---

[3] J. Wash Watts. *A Survey of Old Testament Teaching Vol. 1* (Nashville, Tennessee: Broadman Press, 1947) 27.

[4] Arnold G. Fruchtenbaum. *The Book of Genesis* (San Antonio, Texas: Ariel Ministries, 2009) 77.

literally found in the 'dust of the earth.'"[5] From the pages of Scripture, many truths concerning man can be ascertained. God took special interest in creating man. Of all God's other creations, more information is given concerning the creation of man and his designed purpose. Why did man stand apart from the animals? He alone was created in the 'image and likeness of God' (Genesis 1:27). This "establishes a personal relationship between God and man that does not exist with any other aspect of creation."[6] Man was created and designed to have and enjoy an intimate and personal relationship with God. God *spoke* creation into existence (Psalm 33:6); but, God *made* man from the dust of the earth. God is a personal and intimate God!

Only of man is it written that the LORD God breathed life into man, making him a living soul (Genesis 2:7). Man was not only a physical being, but now was also a spiritual being. "In his nature, person, and personality, in his moral and spiritual capacities, in his emotions, intellect, conscience, and will, man stands apart from the brute creation."[7] In the Semitic world, the act of naming something, or someone, was evidence of lordship. God named the man Adam. The second character within this narrative is now introduced. "And God saw everything He had made, and, behold, it was very good" (Genesis 1:31).

"And the LORD God took the man, and put him in the garden of Eden to dress and keep it" (Genesis 2:15). Adam was given the responsibility to cultivate and maintain the garden. He was given work to do, before he recognized it as work! As the LORD placed Adam in this garden, He issued a directive and a command to Adam. Adam was instructed that the fruit of every tree was his to freely eat, except the fruit of the tree of knowledge of good and evil. Death would be the consequence for disobeying the LORD's command. Without such a

---

[5] Bill Sheffield, *The Beginnings Under Attack* (Springfield, Missouri: 21st Century Press, 2003), 67.

[6] John MacArthur. *The Macarthur Bible Commentary* (Nashville, Tennessee: Thomas Nelson, Inc., 2005) 11.

[7] John Phillips. *Exploring Genesis: An Expository Commentary* (Grand Rapids, Michigan: Kregel Publications, 1980), 45.

necessary choice and the power to choose, Adam could not have been a moral, accountable being.

One may pose the question, "How did Adam know that *death* would be a punishment?" Death had not yet been experienced or witnessed. The Scriptures do not provide an answer for us. However, in speculation, Adam was no Neanderthal. His intellectual genius is unsurpassed; the most brilliant minds today pale in comparison to Adam's.

Adam did not grow or evolve into a man; God created a full grown man. From the moment Adam was created, he possessed complete command of his mental and physical faculties. He had the ability to stand upright and walk. To Adam, God gave dominion over the fish of the sea, fowl of the air, all animal life, and dominion over all the earth (Genesis 1:26). Adam was instructed to subdue and populate the earth. He was God's representative to rule the earth.

Adam demonstrated his lordship over the animal life when he gave names to all the "beasts of the field and every fowl of the air" (Genesis 2:19). It was this event that caused Adam to become consciously aware that there was no other of God's creation like him. Adam was alone! There was no other creature to which Adam could relate. Referring to the aloneness of Adam was the first time during creation God said that something was 'not good'. "And the LORD God said, It is not good that man should be alone; I will make him an help meet for him" (Genesis 2:18). Take note, God is going to *make* Adam a help meet.

As a deep sleep came upon Adam, God took a rib from Adam's side. From this rib, God formed the first woman to be loved, protected, and provided for, by Adam. When God presented her to Adam as his wife and completer, they united and became as one. The three of them, God, Adam, and his help meet (who was not yet named) began to enjoy a wonderful life together. The LORD came daily to the Garden of Eden, this place of perfection, to commune with His beloved creations. Their attribute of innocence allowed fellowship between them and Holy God. Phillips offers the following insight concerning the distinctiveness of man:

Physically, he alone of all the creatures on the globe, walks uprightly; mentally, he alone has the ability to communicate in a sophisticated manner; spiritually, he alone has the capacity to know the mind and will of God ... God crowned man by bestowing upon him posterity—"Be fruitful and multiply" (1:28a) ... with a position (1:28b) giving him dominion over the fish of the sea, over the fowl of the air, and over every living thing ... and with a possession (1:29-32); He gave him a paradise to enjoy.[8]

Adam and his help meet enjoyed a peaceful and tranquil life within the perfect and blissful environment of Eden. This first couple lived in harmony with each other. There existed nothing to cause stress, arguments, or problems between them. They lived without shame, for the Bible says, "they were both naked, the man and his wife, and were not ashamed" (Genesis 2:25). Neither had been exposed to anything that would distort, or dement, their minds with lustful or evil thoughts. "Before the fall, Adam and Eve were both naked ... and not ashamed. The idea of "nakedness" is far more than mere nudity. It has the sense of being totally open and exposed as a person before God and man. To be naked ... and not ashamed means you have no sin, nothing to be rightly ashamed of, nothing to hide."[9] (Note that in the above quote, Adam's help meet is called Eve. However, Eve was not given her name until Genesis 3:20 and in this chronological narrative, that time has not yet arrived.)

The Bible does not provide any time frame, but the first couple continued to obediently fulfill their God given task to *dress* and *keep* the garden. Adam was given the task of working the garden as a service to God. It was also Adam's responsibility to keep, or guard, the garden.

---

[8] Phillips, *Exploring Genesis: An Expository Commentary*, 45-46.

[9] David Guzik. "Study Guide for Genesis 2." Enduring Word. Blue Letter Bible. 7 Jul 2006. 2013. 29 Mar2013.<http://www.blueletterbible.org/commentaries/comm_view.cfm?AuthorID=2&contentID=7322&commInfo=31&topic=Genesis&ar=Gen_2_25 > (accessed March 29, 2013).

"The emphasis here is that he is to guard the Garden of Eden, not in the sense of any external enemies, but rather to guard it in the sense of obeying the commandment of God."[10] The Scriptures affirm that each day, "in the cool of the day" (Genesis 3:8), God would come to the Garden and commune with Adam and his wife. Life was great!

One fateful day, everything changed! The third chapter of the Book of Genesis not only provides details of the cataclysmic day for humanity, but also reveals the love and grace of God for mankind. Without a good understanding of this chapter, it would be difficult, if not impossible, to understand the remainder of the Bible. It is in this chapter the need for redemption is found and God's plan for redeeming man begins to unfold with the first foreshadow of the Lamb.

Chapter three of Genesis begins by introducing another important character to the narrative, the serpent. "Now the serpent was more subtle than any beast of the field which the LORD God had made" (Genesis 3:1a). Though this reference to the serpent is of a literal serpent, it is also symbolic of Satan. Satan not only uses the serpent as an instrument to do his bidding, but actually indwells the serpent enabling communication between the serpent and the woman. However, Fruchtenbaum reveals that Jewish rabbinic tradition teaches that the serpent was created to be elevated above the other creatures of creation as a servant of mankind with the power of speech and the ability to walk upright.[11] The New Testament provides substantial evidence that the serpent and Satan were acting as one: 2 Corinthians 11:3; Revelation 12:9; and Revelation 20:2. The term 'subtle' means wise, crafty, or shrewd. "Shrewdness manifests intelligence, but it is such intelligence as can be prostituted to evil purposes. Craftiness manifests skill and art, but such art as may be deceitful and destructive."[12] The subtlety with which the serpent was created, Satan used for a sinful purpose.

Who is Satan and where did he come from? In Isaiah 14:12-15 and again in Ezekiel 28:11-15, it is revealed that Satan is a fallen angel and a

---

[10] Arnold G. Fruchtenbaum. *The Book of Genesis* (San Antonio, Texas: Ariel Ministries, 2009) 79.

[11] Ibid. 93.

[12] J. Wash Watts. *A Survey of Old Testament Teaching Vol. 1.* 30.

pronounced enemy to God. This angel was originally created as Lucifer, which means 'the bright one', or 'son of the morning' (Isaiah 14:12). It is believed by some theologians that Lucifer could have been one of the three archangels of God's heaven, as he was one of three angels named in Scripture, along with Michael and Gabriel. Some believe each archangel ruled over a third of heaven's angels. Lucifer witnessed heaven's beauty and God's glory firsthand. In Ezekiel 28:12b, one finds a descriptive reference to Lucifer, "Thus saith the LORD God; Thou sealest up the sum, full of wisdom, and perfect in beauty." In the same chapter, Lucifer is recognized as one that was created as " … the anointed cherub that covereth" (Ezekiel 28:14a). It is understood that Lucifer occupied a special place of prominence as a guardian of the throne of God. Ezekiel continues by revealing Lucifer was perfect in his ways from the day he was created until iniquity was found in him, verse 15.

What caused Lucifer, such a perfect, beautiful, and wise creature, to allow iniquity into his heart and disrupt the harmony of heaven? According to Isaiah 14:13-14, it was pride and a desire to act independently of God! These verses relate five "I wills" of Lucifer: "*I will* ascend into heaven … *I will* exalt my throne above the stars of God … *I will* sit also upon the mount of the congregation … *I will* ascend above the heights of the clouds", and "*I will* be like the most High", (italics mine). What arrogance of a being created by Almighty God, created to serve Almighty God! As a result of his iniquity, God removed Lucifer from his prominent position, stripped him of his heavenly rank, and threw him out of heaven! However, Lucifer was able to deceive one third of the angelic hosts (possibly the third of the angels over which he ruled) to follow him, and they, too, were thrown out of heaven. Lucifer was now Satan, also known as the devil, the pronounced hater and enemy of God. Ultimately, Satan is a defeated foe with an eternity within the lake of fire awaiting him. "Yet thou shalt be brought down to hell, to the sides of the pit" (Isaiah 14:15). "And the devil that deceived them was cast into the lake of fire and brimstone, where the beast and the false prophet are, and shall be tormented day and night for ever and ever" (Revelation 20:10). But until that day, he attempts to defile and destroy everything associated with Holy God. The beauty and wisdom that Lucifer had was not lost, but was definitely corrupted. Thus, Satan began his devious attack against God's crowning creation—Man.

Satan, through the serpent, first approached the woman with a question intending to create doubt in her mind concerning the command of God, "Yea, hath God said, ye shall not eat of every tree of the garden?" (Genesis 3:1b). A command that God had made very clear was now presented in a manner as to create debate. This is much the same way a liberal theologian approaches God's Word! One must remember, the initial commands from God were given to Adam before the creation of his help meet. So, her knowledge had been acquired through oral communication with Adam. This could possibly be one of the reasons Satan first approached the woman, instead of Adam. The woman's response to Satan's question reveals she clearly understood God's command, "We may eat of the fruit of the trees of the garden. But of the fruit of the tree which is in the midst of the garden, God hath said, Ye shall not eat of it, neither shall ye touch it, lest ye die" (Genesis 3:2-3). Her addition of the words, "neither shall ye touch it", may simply indicate her recognition of the strictness of the prohibition of eating the fruit of the tree of knowledge of good and evil.

Secondly, Satan approaches the woman with a clear denial of God's consequences of disobedience to His command. Satan told her, "Ye shall not surely die" (Genesis 3:4). God's integrity was clearly under attack. The woman may have been enticed by Satan to first simply touch the fruit. In so doing, Satan could have convinced her that she would not die and that God wanted to keep her and Adam from obtaining the knowledge which would enable them to become like God. The woman was tempted in the three ways as described in 1 John 2:16, "the lust of the flesh, and the lust of the eyes, and the pride of life."

Being tempted was not the sin, but sin entered when the forbidden fruit was willfully taken and eaten. The woman then gave to Adam and he knowingly disobeyed the command of God and ate of the fruit. Satan had succeeded in deceiving Adam and his wife to do as he once did—act independently and in disobedience to God! The Bible clarifies that the woman was deceived, but that Adam disobeyed with full knowledge, 1 Timothy 2:13-14 and 2 Corinthians 11:3. The plural pronoun, 'we', in Genesis 3:2, seems to indicate that Adam was present at the scene and in full knowledge of the dialogue between the woman and the serpent. Adam, as the God appointed head of the home, should have assumed his responsibility, intervened, and stopped the dialogue between his wife and the serpent. Unfortunately, Adam stood passively by and became an accessory to the sin. "Whatever the fruit may have been, its use was a plain violation of divine prohibition, an unwarranted desire for forbidden knowledge. The gravity of the offense consisted, not only in the act itself, but in the fact that Adam and Eve committed it consciously and deliberately against God's explicit and emphatic command."[13] (Note: in the above quote, Adam's help meet is called Eve, who was not named until the third chapter of Genesis, verse 20, and in this chronological narrative that time has not arrived). Adam carries the responsibility for the condition of mankind, for God had placed him as head of the human race. "Wherefore, as by one man sin entered into the world, and death by sin; and so death passed upon all men, for that all have sinned" (Romans 5:12).

So, what transpired when Adam and his help meet disobeyed God and sinned against Him? Everything changed! But the first change, and the most detrimental, was that they both experienced a spiritual death. Immediately, they came under the penalty of their sin; "the wages of sin is death … " (Romans 6:23a). Therefore, the consequence of the original sin was that at the moment Adam ate the forbidden fruit he would die (Genesis 2:17). Although Adam lived to be nine hundred and thirty years old, he did eventually experience *physical* death (Genesis 5:5). However, he and his wife immediately died *spiritually* at the moment they sinned and this penalty would be transmitted to his children and their progeny. Simply and to the point, all born thereafter are descendants of Adam and Eve and are under the curse of death and all are born spiritually dead in sin and under the wrath of God! Man now needed a Savior!

---

[13] Spiros Zodhiates. *The Hebrew-Greek Key Study Bible* (Grand Rapides, Michigan: Baker Book House, 1984) 5; notes on verses 3:1-7.

The Bible states, "And the eyes of them both were opened, and they knew that they were naked; and they sewed fig leaves together, and made themselves aprons" (Genesis 3:7). What originally was an indication of innocence and a sign of a healthy union, now became a sign of shame. Phillips offers the following interesting observation concerning the nakedness of Adam and his help meet, or Eve, as she was later named:

> Before the fall, Adam and Eve were probably clothed with light, because God covers Himself with light as with a garment (Psalm 104:2) and because the Lord Jesus, in His transfiguration, was similarly arrayed (Mark 9:2-3). The moment they sinned, Adam and Eve saw the light go out. The death of the spirit within them caused the light to be extinguished and, suddenly, the physical side of their being was thrust into a prominence it had never been before. They knew they were naked.[14]

Now, in their confused state of mind, Adam and his help meet pathetically attempted to replace the radiant garments of their innocence and cover the shame of their nakedness by making aprons of sewn together fig leaves. They were oblivious to the reality that it was their naked soul which needed to be confessed to God and covered, not their physical naked bodies. Sin not only affected the relationship between Adam and his wife, but also affected every relationship; most importantly, their relationship with God.

In the cool of the day, God came to the garden as He regularly did, seeking the communion with Adam and the woman. When the now sinful couple heard Holy God walking in the garden, they hid in fear. A once joyfully anticipated, transparent, and guilt free fellowship with Holy God was now paralyzed with fear—broken and hindered because of willful, sinful disobedience. It was the LORD who personally took the initiative and came seeking Adam and his wife. The Bible makes

---

[14] Phillips, *Exploring Genesis: An Expository Commentary*, 59.

abundantly clear it is not man who initially seeks God, but God seeks man! "There is none that understandeth, there is none that seeketh after God" (Romans 3:11). Later in the New Testament, one reads, "For the Son of man is come to seek and to save that which was lost" (Luke 19:10). Man is simply called to come to Him in repentance, responding to God's invitation for salvation.

Omniscient God knew where the couple was hiding, yet He called for them, questioning their location. All-knowing God confronted Adam and brought him to acknowledge his sin. Sin had severed the closeness of fellowship between man and God. The consequences of disobedience had been pre-disclosed; therefore, judgment and justice had to be rendered. Judgment was death, spiritual and physical. Spiritual death, separation of the union between God and man, was immediate; physical death was yet to come.

Adam, the woman, and the serpent fell under the curse of sin and God informed each of them the consequences of their disobedience. God dealt severely with the serpent for his deceitful actions in the deception of the woman. The serpent lost his prominent position among the animal kingdom, being cursed above all. From that day forward, the serpent would no longer be capable of walking upright, but would slither across the ground eating its dust.

God clearly explained to Adam and his help meet the consequences of their disobedient actions. He informed them their lives would never be the same because of their sin. The woman would henceforth experience tremendous pain in childbearing and she would become subject to her husband's authority. It was then that Adam exercised his authority and gave his help meet her name, Eve, which means 'mother of all living' (Genesis 3:20). Adam would experience toilsome labor to provide food for his family, for the ground was now cursed and would not easily produce, and Adam would battle weeds, thorns, and thistles. His work would change from a joyful experience to a burdensome task and for the first time in his existence he would wipe sweat from his brow. Both Adam and Eve were informed they would one day experience physical death and return to the ground from whence they came.

Before the foundations of the world, God, in His infinite knowledge, knew man would sin. God looked through the portals of time and saw mankind's greatest need. He would need a way back to God! Man would need a Savior! Holy God could have chosen to annihilate man's existence, which he deserved, and start all over; but, instead God demonstrated His divine love and grace. Though God knew Adam and Eve had sinned, He still sought them and He initiated the approach. This presents a beautiful picture of God's love and concern for lost humanity.

It was at this moment the first messianic prophecy was spoken by God concerning the coming of man's redeemer and Satan's defeat. God declared to Satan through the serpent, "And I will put enmity between thee and the woman, and between thy seed and her seed; it shall bruise thy head, and thou shalt bruise his heel" (Genesis 3:15). The 'seed of the woman' refers to the supernatural conception of the Messiah Himself. The third chapter of Genesis reveals the origin of humanity's sin and the divine purpose of the Messiah's coming to deal with the problem of humanity's sin in an act of amazing grace!

Scripture presents God's amazing act of grace and His divine provision on behalf of Adam and Eve. "Unto Adam also and to his wife did the LORD God make coats of skins, and clothed them" (Genesis 3:21). God reveals His personal touch once again when He *made* coats of skin as a proper covering for Adam and Eve. These coats of skins came from animals, which required the death and the shedding of blood of the animals. This was the first blood sacrifice made in the context of judgment of sin. The blood sacrifice provided atonement for the sin of Adam and Eve. These coats of skin provided an acceptable covering of their shame and nakedness, replacing their covering of fig leaves.

The Prophet Isaiah teaches us the necessity of atonement. Atonement, 'covering', is provided only by a blood sacrifice. The correlation between the shed blood and the acceptable covering is depicted in Isaiah 61:10, "I will greatly rejoice in the LORD, my soul shall be joyful in my God; for he hath clothed me with the *garments of salvation*, he hath covered me with the *robe of righteousness*, as a bridegroom decketh himself with ornaments, and as a bride adorneth herself with her jewels", (italics mine). The glorified Lord addressed this covering as " ... *white raiment,* that thou mayest be clothed, and that the shame of thy nakedness do not appear" (Revelation 3:18b), (italics mine).

Adam and Eve witnessed their first experience with death when God shed the blood of the innocent animal. They were becoming painfully aware of the tremendous price for their transgression. God demonstrated His love and expressed His grace, presenting the first gospel message to Adam and Eve. In descriptive pictorial language, He explained the important significance of the blood sacrifice needed for the remission of sin. The sin could be forgiven, but the price still had to be paid! God also taught them of the substitutionary sacrifice which was essential to maintain fellowship with Him. One that was guilty could not pay the price for another that was guilty. It would take 'One' who was innocent to pay the debt for the guilty! This act of sacrifice became a constant reminder of man's sinfulness and need for redemption. Whereas this sacrifice was temporary and merely *covered* the sin, it did not *take away* the sin. This blood sacrifice foreshadowed the permanent work of redemption that was to come. What animal gave its life to provide coats of skin for Adam and Eve? According to Proverbs 27:26a, it could have been an innocent defenseless lamb: "The lambs are for thy clothing." This is the first foreshadow of the 'Lamb of God'! This is the 'Alpha Lamb'!

Now, in a compassionate act of grace, God expelled Adam and Eve from the Garden of Eden. Had Adam and Eve eaten of the tree of life after their sin, they would have lived forever physically in a state of sinfulness. There was danger in allowing them access to the tree of life: "lest he put forth his hand, and take also of the tree of life, and eat, and live forever" (Genesis 3:22b). God drove Adam and Eve from the Garden and they began to experience life as God never intended for them to experience—knowing good and evil. Paradise was lost! They took with them the precious memories of the sweet fellowship with God, which now was severed by their sin. However, they also took with them the message of atonement through the shedding of blood, which they continually practiced and taught to their children as the way to fellowship with God. One can imagine they daily longed to return to

Paradise; they longed for permanent removal of their sin; and longed for reconciliation through the Lamb!

Each day, Adam and Eve, may have longingly gazed at the entrance of the Garden, reminiscent of the wonderful life they had forfeited. The Cherubim, placed there by God to prohibit entrance into the Garden and to deny access to the tree of life, was a constant reminder there was nothing they could do to regain entrance into that beautiful, serene place.

When Adam and Eve's first son, Cain, was born, Eve may have thought he was the fulfillment of the prophetic statement of God. "And I will put enmity between thee and the woman, and between thy seed and her seed; it shall bruise thy head, and thou shalt bruise his heel" (Genesis 3:15). Cain's name carries the meaning, "I have gotten a man from the LORD" (Genesis 3:24b). However, it would not take very long for them to see evidence that Cain was not the prophesied Savior, or Messiah. Later, the couple had another son, Abel, (Genesis 4:2).

The family may have made regular visits to the Garden's entrance. There, Adam may have described the beauty of the Garden and the fellowship he and Eve had once enjoyed with God. Then, with a broken and repentant heart, Adam possibly recounted the events to his sons of the regretful day he and their mother yielded to the subtle temptation of the master deceiver and opened the door to sin. Possibly continuing with great remorse, Adam described the dreadful cost of that sin: the broken fellowship with God, the shame, plunging all of mankind into sin, and paradise lost. God had warned them of the consequences of their disobedience: death would be the result. Then, with rejoicing reverberating within his voice, Adam could have described the amazing grace of God as the Lord came to them, offering reconciliation and forgiveness of their sin. In vivid detail, Adam could have related to his sons the sacrificial act that God Himself offered on behalf of their undeserving parents. Adam could have explained to his sons the purpose of the innocent lamb that was slain, why its blood was spilled as an atonement for their sin, and how its skin was taken as a covering for their shame. God had instructed Adam of the essentiality of the shedding of blood for the remission of their sin. Since that day, Adam and Eve, could have periodically offered a blood sacrifice as the form of worship to God and as a reminder of their need for His grace. This may possibly have been done on the anniversary of the tragic event of their expulsion from the Garden.

The Scripture relates that in the process of time both Cain and Abel brought an offering to the Lord. "And in the process of time it came to pass, that Cain brought of the fruit of the ground and offering unto the LORD. And Abel, he also brought of the firstlings of his flock and of the fat thereof. And the LORD had respect unto Abel and to his offering; but unto Cain and to his offering he had not respect" (Genesis 4:3-5a). Cain, being a tiller of the ground had chosen to bring as his offering the fruit and vegetables of his crop. Abel, a shepherd, presented to God the best of his flock, a blood sacrifice. The Scripture states Cain's sacrifice was not received, but Abel's was. Why was Cain's offering rejected by God, but Abel's was accepted? Cain, most likely, offered the best of his harvest, for which he was most proud. His motives may have been sincere when he presented his offering unto the LORD, but it revealed the attitude of unbelief within his heart. A bloodless offering was not inappropriate as an offering of thanksgiving, but was unacceptable as a sin offering. Cain did not approach God in faith, as did Abel, his brother. One is warned not to approach God in the same manner as Cain, as revealed in 1 John 3:12, "Not as Cain, who was of that wicked one, and slew his brother. And wherefore slew he him? Because his own works were evil, and his brother's righteous."

Abel came in faith, believing the truth taught to him by his parents that only by a blood sacrifice could atonement for sin be made. "By faith Abel offered unto God a more excellent sacrifice than Cain, by which he obtained witness that he was righteous, God testifying of his gifts: ... " (Hebrews 11:4). Unfortunately, Cain did as his father before him. Remember, Adam attempted to cover himself and his shame with the fig leaves. Likewise, Cain attempted himself to cover his sin. "Cain is promised restored fellowship if he does well; but, if not, the effects of *sin* are ready to pounce (*lieth*) on him. Sin is pictured as a demon ready to pounce on Cain to enslave him."[15] The Scripture warns, "There is a way that seemeth right unto man, but the end thereof are the ways of death" (Proverbs 14:12). When one rejects God's provision for acceptance to Himself through the blood sacrifice, it is described in Jude 11 as, "the way of Cain". Today's equivalent would be the rejection of God's offer of forgiveness through Christ.

Through the 'Alpha Lamb', God had taught Adam and Eve and they had taught their sons that to all descendants of Adam and Eve would Adam's sin be imputed. Justice must be rendered and without the shedding of blood there would be no atonement for sin. Through a repentant heart, the offering was to be presented in obedient faith. This was to be the offering for atonement and the proper approach to Holy God. This was God's prescribed manner of offering and nothing but the blood would suffice! This truth was verbally communicated throughout the generations and this is how men, such as Noah and Abraham, became knowledgeable to offer sacrifice to Holy God and the type of offering that would be accepted.

Observe the parallels of the spiritual truths between the 'Alpha Lamb' and the 'Lamb of God':

1) The innocent would be the substitute for the guilty. God made the 'Lamb of God' who knew no sin, to become sin for us, (2 Corinthians 5:17a).

2) One must have a proper covering. Through the 'Lamb of God' man can receive the righteousness of God, (2 Corinthians 5:17b).

3) The man-made covering was not acceptable. " ... our righteousnesses are as filthy rags ... " (Isaiah 64:6); "Not by works of righteousness which we have done, but according to his mercy he saved us ... " (Titus 3:5a).

---

[15] Charles Ryrie. *Ryrie Study Bible, King James Version*. Chicago, Illinois: Moody Publishers, 1986, 1994. 10. notes on Genesis 4:7.

4) God Himself must provide the covering. "For by grace are ye saved through faith; and that not of yourselves: it is the gift of God: not of works, lest any man should boast" (Ephesians 2:8-9).

5) The proper covering required the shedding of blood. " ... it is the blood that maketh an atonement for the soul" (Leviticus 17:11b); "In whom we have redemption through his blood, the forgiveness of sins, according to the riches of his grace" (Ephesians 1:7).

6) God's grace provided the covering for them before they were expelled from the garden. Before man was ever created, God had a plan of redemption in place to reconcile man back to Himself, (Ephesians 1:3-12).

Let's continue the journey in the book of Genesis and ponder the truths revealed by the next foreshadow the story of Abraham and Isaac. Would your faith be strong enough to obey a command to offer your son as a sacrifice?

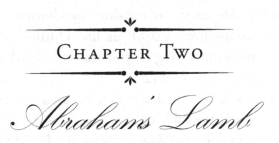

CHAPTER TWO

Abraham's Lamb

In the preceding chapter, an account is given at the beginning of humanity of the 'Alpha Lamb' as the first sacrifice to atone for the sin of man. This sacrifice was offered in an unblemished garden. As the journey continues the second foreshadow is revealed; it will be shocking to discover that this sacrifice is not an animal sacrifice! This will connect and illumine the truth of an acceptable sacrifice. This sacrifice is presented on a desolate mountain top and involves a man through whom another race of people will evolve, the chosen people of God—the Hebrews.

The Scripture records the life of a man named Abram born approximately two thousand to twenty-five hundred years after Adam. It is within his life and the life of his son, Isaac, one discovers the most poignant account of the second foreshadow of the Lamb of God, 'Abraham's Lamb'. In the twenty-second chapter of the book of Genesis, God presents the reader a very descriptive revelation of His redemptive plan and the love, agony, and obedience involved.

Before this epic event is unfolded, one must look at the miraculous life of this man named Abram. Abram is introduced in Genesis 11:26-32 as the son of a man named Terah. There are not many details concerning Terah who, with his family, moved from his home in a place named Ur of the Chaldees, to a place called Haran approximately six hundred miles southeast. Both places, Haran and Ur of the Chaldees, were towns of the Babylonian Empire which were devoted worshippers of the moon god. According to Joshua 24:2, " … Terah, the father of Abraham, the father of Nachor: and they served other gods." Terah was himself a worshipper of the heathen gods. It was in this pagan environment that Abram, one of the three sons born to Terah, possibly lived the first seventy-five years of his life. During this time frame, Abram wed a beautiful young lady named Sarai, who was actually Abram's half sister, Genesis 20:12.

After his father's death, Abram first received the gracious call to follow Jehovah God. The Bible tells us in Genesis 12:1-3 of God's call, instruction, and promise to Abram. "Now the LORD had said unto Abram, Get thee out of thy country, and from thy kindred, and from thy father's house, unto a land that I will shew thee: And I will make of thee a great nation, and I will bless thee, and make thy name great; and thou shalt be a blessing: And I will bless them that bless thee, and curse him that curseth thee: and in thee shall all families of the earth be blessed." God's call to Abram brought him out of the pagan culture of idolatry. The LORD instructed Abram to follow Him to another land where He promised to bless Abram. God promised to make Abram's name great. Abram, whose name was later changed to Abraham, is mentioned three hundred and twelve times in two hundred and seventy-two verses in the Bible. He is certainly one of the most well known men in the Old Testament and one of the most influential men in history. God promised to make a great nation out of Abram's descendants. This would be the birth of the Hebrew nation, known now as Israel. The promise of God included protection and that through the descendants of Abram all other families would be blessed. This promise was remarkable, for Abram and his wife, Sarai, were childless—Sarai was barren.

Abram, as Noah who lived centuries before, found grace in the sight of the LORD in the midst of a perverse and wicked environment. Genesis 15:6 describes the heart and attitude of Abram toward the LORD: "And he believed in the LORD; and he counted it to him for righteousness." If one traces back through the ancestry of Abram, one will discover men of strong faith in God; men like Shem, the son of

Noah, who was still living at the time of Abram. Could it have been that the message of redemption passed down through the generations by these great men of faith had penetrated the heart and mind of Abram? "Thus Abram's pilgrimage began where ours begins, with a vision of another country, a better country, a home forever blessed as the dwelling place of God. God speaks, we believe, faith dawns, life begins."[16]

How did Abram become a man of great faith in God? Throughout Abram's life, he had his faith in God repeatedly tested as he learned to trust the Word of God. His walk of faith began as every other believer: walking in the light, or knowledge, he had been given while waiting on new light, or knowledge, and direction. Abram's faith was initially tested when he was called by God to leave his homeland. At the age of seventy-five, Abram took his wife, left his father and family and began his journey to a land that God said He would show him. It wasn't until Abram arrived in the land of Canaan that God appeared unto him and promised to give the land of Canaan to Abram's descendants. Upon receiving this message, Abram built an altar and worshipped the Lord. "And the LORD appeared unto Abram, and said, Unto thy seed will I give this land: and there builded he and altar unto the LORD, who appeared unto him" (Genesis 12:7). Although, the land was occupied by the ungodly Canaanites, Abram did not rely upon his human faculties to bring to fruition God's promise and plan. Instead, Abram began to personify the Scriptures later recorded in Proverbs 3:5-6, "Trust in the LORD with all thine heart; and lean not unto thine own understanding. In all thy ways acknowledge him, and he shall direct thy paths."

Again, Abram was tested as he sojourned throughout the unfamiliar land. Soon, a famine overpowered the land of Canaan. Still young in his faith, Abram turned to Egypt to provide for him and his family. Abram and Sarai found themselves in a land where the Pharaoh could do as he pleased. This included taking beautiful women into his harem. Sarai was a beautiful woman at the age of sixty-five, but based upon the longevity of her life, she was a middle aged woman, for she lived to be one hundred and twenty-seven. Abram feared for his life thinking that

---

[16] Phillips, *Exploring Genesis: An Expository Commentary*, 115.

Pharaoh would kill him in order to take Sarai into his harem. Abram allowed fear to control him and consorted with Sarai concerning their relationship. She was to conceal the fact that she was Abram's wife and answer any inquiry that she was his sister. Though Sarai was Abram's half-sister, she and Abram should not have misled Pharaoh. Pharaoh took Sarai, but the Lord plagued Pharaoh because of Sarai. It is the belief of this writer this plague prevented any intimacy to transpire between Pharaoh and Sarai. Abram's lie and deceit were discovered, but God delivered Sarai from Pharaoh. Abram and his family left Egypt and returned to Canaan and worshipped at the altar he had built in Bethel, Genesis 13:3-4. Abram was maturing in his faith and learning to trust in the Lord and not in his own understanding.

There were many other tests throughout Abram's life; some he had to experience more than once. Often, it takes God several times to teach one the lesson He desires to teach. Abram's next major test was learning to trust in God's ability to bring to fruition His promises in His own time. It had been several years since God had promised Abram an heir. Abram grew anxious, due to his age, that he remained childless. He had contemplated incorporating an acceptable practice of his time, which was to adopt one of his servants, Eliezer, to become his heir. However, God stopped Abram and reiterated His promise and clearly stated that Abram would have a son. "He that shall come from thine own bowels shall be thine heir" (Genesis 15:4).

At the age of eighty-five, Abram still remained childless! Sarai made a proposal to Abram that was in accordance to the laws of their time. According to the *Nuzi Tablets* and the *Code of Hammurabi*, "if a wife proved to be barren, she was obligated to provide to her husband a *handmaid* through whom he could have children so that his seed does not die out."[17] Children born in this manner would become officially and legally the children of the mistress. Even if the laws of the land allow certain activities and practices, a child of God must direct his life according to God's truths and the principles of righteousness. Though God had not specified that Sarai was to be the mother of

---

[17] Fruchtenbaum, *The Book of Genesis*, 286.

Abram's heir, she should have concluded that fact, as she was Abram's only wife. Unfortunately, this proved to be a lapse of faith for both Sarai and Abram. Sarai offered Abram her handmaid, Hagar, and he accepted. "Now Sarai Abram's wife bare him no children: and she had an handmaid, an Egyptian, whose name was Hagar. And Sarai said unto Abram, Behold now, the LORD hath restrained me from bearing: I pray thee, go in unto my maid; it may be that I may obtain children by her. And Abram hearkened to the voice of Sarai" (Genesis 16:1-2). This was definitely a failure to trust God to bring to fruition His promise through the natural and normal course of events. Hagar was an Egyptian maidservant and Abram and Sarai seemed to have acquired her as a handmaiden through Pharaoh, Genesis 12:16. The following year, when Abram was eighty-six years old, Ishmael was born to Hagar. However, Ishmael was not the son that God had promised to give to Abram. "And as for Ishmael, I have heard thee: Behold, I have blessed him, and will make him fruitful, and will multiply him exceedingly; twelve princes shall he beget, and I will make him a great nation. But my covenant will I establish with Isaac, which Sarah shall bear unto thee at this set time next year" (Genesis 17:20-21). Within the spiritual growth process, one must take responsibility for one's mistakes and learn from them.

It was not until Abram was ninety-nine years old that God visited him and clearly promised that he and Sarai would have the promised son—Isaac. At this time, God changed the name of Abram to Abraham. One finds this chronicled in Genesis 17:5, "Neither shall thy name any more be called Abram, but thy name shall be Abraham; for a father of many nations have I made thee." Abram meant 'exalted father', whereas, Abraham carries the meaning of 'father of many'. God also changed Sarai's name to Sarah. "And God said unto Abraham, As for Sarai thy wife, thou shalt not call her name Sarai, but Sarah shall her name be" (Genesis 17:15). Marking the significance of the occasion, her name now carried the meaning of 'princess'.

Throughout this journey, Abraham learned to solely trust the Word of the Lord. Abraham's faith and trust in God would be graciously rewarded with the birth of Isaac. With each test, Abraham's faith continued to mature. The New Testament reveals, "that the trial of your faith, being much more precious than of gold that perisheth, though it be tried with fire, might be unto the praise and honour and glory at the appearing of Jesus Christ" (1 Peter 1:7).

When Abraham was ninety-nine years old and his wife, Sarah, was ninety, God again visited Abraham and confirmed His promise of an heir—the promised son, Isaac. "And God said, Sarah thy wife shall bear thee a son indeed; and thou shalt call his name Isaac: and I will establish my covenant with him for an everlasting covenant, and with his seed after him ... But my covenant will I establish with Isaac, which Sarah shall bear unto thee at this set time next year" (Genesis 17:19, 21). When Abraham was one hundred years old and Sarah was well past her child bearing days, the miraculous birth of the promised son occurred. This was indeed an epic day in the life of Abraham. The heir through whom the covenant of God would be fulfilled had been born!

The birth of Isaac was a foreshadow of the miraculous birth of the future Messiah, the Lamb of God. As Isaac was born by the power of God's Spirit, Galatians 4:29, so was the Lamb of God, the Son of many promises, or prophesies, Micah 5:2. Just as the birth of Isaac took place at God's set time, Genesis 17:21; so the Lamb of God was sent in the "fullness of time" (Galatians 4:4).

Abraham and Sarah were ecstatic over the arrival of their son, Isaac. "And Sarah said, God had made me to laugh, so that all that hear will laugh with me" (Genesis 21:6); Isaac's name means 'laughter'. This was definitely a very joyous occasion! In the years following, one can imagine how Abraham reveled in the joys of fatherhood, loving and nurturing his young sons, Ishmael and Isaac, instructing and teaching them to honor and obey Almighty God. Abraham proudly watched his sons mature into strong, young men. Observing Abraham's faith and obedience to God, Isaac alone began to emulate his father's faith.

As Isaac and Ishmael grew, there arose strife and jealousy between them and their mothers. Sarah's attitude had changed toward Hagar soon after the birth of Ishmael and Sarah began treating Hagar harshly, Genesis 16:6. Ironically, here the Hebrew was afflicting the Egyptian. In a few years, the Egyptians would be afflicting the Hebrews. When

Ishmael was a young teenager, Sarah wanted Hagar to take her son and leave. Thus, Sarah coaxed Abraham to force Hagar to do so. "And Sarah saw the son of Hagar the Egyptian, which she had born unto Abraham, mocking. Wherefore, she said unto Abraham, Cast out this bondwoman and her son: for the son of this bondwoman shall not be heir with my son, even with Isaac" (Genesis 21:9-10).

Although, Ishmael was not in the design and perfect will of God, God promised to bless Ishmael because of the covenant He had made with Abraham. The LORD promised to make a great nation out the descendants of Ishmael, Genesis 21:13. At the demand of Sarah and because Abraham had been assured by God that Ishmael and Hagar would be taken care of by Him, Abraham sent them away. From Ishmael came the Arab people and nations. From the birth of Isaac, possibly resentment existed within Ishmael. As the sons progressed in years, this resentment evolved into conflict between the two young men and it continues even today among their descendants!

At a specific time in Abraham's life, "And it came to pass after these things ... " (Genesis 22:1a), God challenged Abraham to a supreme test of faith and love for his Lord. After what things? After the things and events that had taken place before this present time; specifically, the other tests of Abraham's faith that God had administered to mature His faith. Abraham had been tested on many occasions, beginning with the Lord's command to leave his homeland and father. Later, Abraham was tested when he surrendered the choice of land to Lot, Genesis 13; he refused to receive the gifts of King Bera of Sodom, Genesis 14:22-24; then, Abraham was asked to surrender Ishmael, Genesis 21:10-14. Each successful test produced a stronger faith in Abraham to the Word of God. Abraham's faith had grown tremendously over the years he had lived for God. He had learned to trust his God and they had a relationship that was personal and intimate. Abraham was about to be faced with the ultimate test of his life; to surrender his promised son, his 'only begotten son', Isaac, to God as a sacrifice!

The test came when God called His obedient servant, Abraham, and he responded in simple faith; "Behold, here I am" (Genesis 22:1). God issued a specific command to Abraham, "Take now thy son, thine only son, Isaac, whom thou lovest, and get thee into the land of Moriah; and offer him there for a burnt offering upon one of the mountains which I will tell thee of" (Genesis 22:2). "By faith, Abraham, when he was tried, offered up Isaac: and he that had received the promises offered up his only begotten son ... " (Hebrews 11:17).

Wow! A command like that would knock the wind out of most individuals. There was no doubt as to whom God was referring; God had specifically asked that Isaac be the sacrifice. God had, step by step, increasingly identified Isaac as the one He wanted Abraham to sacrifice. Each reference became more painful to Abraham. He loved his son, Isaac, and God knew he did. Some theologians believe that Isaac was a young lad, possibly a teenager. Others believe that Isaac was between twenty and thirty years old, but had yet to be married and had no children. God had promised that "in Isaac shall thy seed be called." Isaac was the promised son! And now God was commanding Abraham to sacrifice his promised son—his heir! Was Abraham going to trust the promise, or the Promiser—God?

Abraham's dilemma was that if he simply trusted the promise, there was a danger of manipulating the situation in order to bring to pass a desired result. Abraham had faced a similar test earlier in his life and the result was the birth of Ishmael to Sarah's handmaid, Hagar. To trust the Promiser, one must allow Him to bring to fruition the promised result in His time and in His way. So, how did Abraham respond to this command of God? Without any apparent hesitation, Abraham obeyed his Lord. "Abraham rose up early in the morning and saddled his ass, and took two of his young men with him, and Isaac his son, and clave the wood for the burnt offering, and rose up, and went unto the place of which God told him" (Genesis 22:3). "Abraham's faithfulness did not take God by surprise. He knew His servant well, but the trial of faith was necessary to mature and develop Abraham's spiritual character."[18]

God directed Abraham to a specific place, Moriah. This was the place where in later years, Solomon would build his Temple in

---

[18] John J. Davis, *Paradise to Prison, Studies in Genesis* (Grand Rapides, Michigan: Baker Book House, 1975), 219.

Jerusalem and where eventually, the Lamb of God, the fulfillment of the foreshadows, would be sacrificed for the sins of all mankind. For three days, Abraham and his company journeyed to Moriah; Isaac walking faithfully and obediently by his father's side. Possibly, throughout these three days Abraham remained unusually quiet, heavy with the weight upon him as he anxiously contemplated what he was about to do!

What father would not have questioned over and over in his mind the command, wanting desperately to make sure he clearly understood his Lord? Every step must have become more and more difficult to take. How could God command such a thing of him? He loved his Lord dearly, but he also loved Isaac. How could he sacrifice his beloved son! Truly, the pain must have torn through his own heart much like the knife would soon be cutting into the flesh of Isaac. Such a burden to bear! Abraham had every intention of obeying the command of God, but it would be the most difficult task he would ever carry out. Obedience is not always painless! This was painful for Abraham, and though possibly fighting back tears, he would be faithful.

On the third day, Abraham and his entourage came to the specific place of God's direction. The two young men unloaded the donkey and began to set up camp. Abraham and Isaac prepared to climb the mountain to worship the Lord. "Mount Moriah represented the highest possible pinnacle of surrender for one and the highest possible sacrifice for the other."[19] Abraham stated his faith in the Promiser, the Lord, when he announced that he and Isaac were going up the mountain to worship and that *both* of them would return. The basis of Abraham's faith was founded in the promise of God in Genesis 21:12, "in Isaac shall thy seed be called." It is later revealed by the writer of Hebrews that although at this time resurrections from the dead were unprecedented, Abraham had faith in God's power to resurrect Isaac in order to fulfill His covenantal promise. "By faith Abraham, when he was tried, offered up Isaac: and that he had received the promises offered up his only begotten son, of whom it was said, that in Isaac shall thy seed be called: accounting that God was able to raise him up, even from the dead; from

---

[19] Phillips, *Exploring Genesis: An Expository Commentary*, 178.

whence also he received him in a figure" (Hebrews 11:17-19). Abraham may have silently prayed, "Lord, I believe, help now my unbelief."

Abraham did not simply state his faith in his Lord; he gave evidence of his faith by his specific actions. This was a personification of what James would later write, "Even so faith, if it hath not works, is dead, being alone. Yea, a man may say, Thou hast faith, and I have works: shew me thy faith without thy works, and I will shew thee my faith by my works" (James 2:17-18). The wood which was prepared for the burnt offering was placed on the back of Isaac. This was the wood upon which Abraham believed his son would soon die. Abraham's hands may have trembled and tears filled his eyes as he strapped the burden of wood to his son's back. Abraham's confidence in his God was unshaken, but his emotions may have been in overdrive. Centuries later, the Lamb of God would carry up this same mountain the wooden cross upon which He would die. Abraham took the fire and the knife as both he and his son went up the mountain. Abraham would sacrifice his son, just as God would one day sacrifice His Son. The Bible states, "they went both of them together" (Genesis 22:6c).

As Isaac obediently walked along beside his father, he observed they had everything for the burnt offering; everything, except a lamb. He asked his father a specific question, "Behold the fire and the wood: but where is the lamb for the burnt offering?" (Genesis 22:7). One would imagine such a question would tear out the heart of Abraham. His beloved son was to be the burnt offering! Abraham was there for the purpose of sacrificing Isaac to God. Agonizing and grief-stricken, he restated his faith in the Lord when he replied to Isaac's question, "My son, God will provide himself a lamb for a burnt offering" (Genesis 22:8a). "In Hebrew, it reads *yireh-lo*, which allows for two options. The first option is that God will provide *for* Himself or, second, that God will provide *Himself* as an offering. It was a divine provision either way."[20] The narrative of Scripture again states, "they went both of them together" (Genesis 22:8b).

---

[20] Fruchtenbaum, *The Book of Genesis*, 354.

The Bible records that "God was in Christ reconciling the world unto himself ... " (2 Corinthians 5:19). The New Testament reveals that the Lamb of God would be forsaken by all who knew Him. Even His most intimate companions would desert Him at His most critical and crucial hour. Yet, the Messiah would state that He was not alone, for His Father was always with Him. Up Moriah, or what later became known as Golgotha, they went *both* of them together.

Abraham and his son came to the designated place and by now, Isaac must have determined the role in which he was to play in the scene that was about to unfold. He could see it in his father's face and hear it in his voice. However, Moriah was not forced upon Isaac. He was a full grown man with strength enough to resist, if he chose to do so. He was not bound and dragged up the mountain; he willingly and obediently surrendered in trusting submissiveness to his father's will. Looking ahead, the Lamb of God would one day speak as He approached His Moriah, "Now my soul is troubled; and what shall I say? Father, save me from this hour: but for this cause came I unto this hour. Father, glorify thy name" (John 12:27-28a). The 'Lamb of God' would willingly surrender to and trust His Father's will.

Isaac observed his father preparing the altar of sacrifice. Isaac possibly assisted his father in arranging the wood. Isaac trusted his father and his obedience to his father was unprecedented. He then submitted himself to his father as he was bound and placed upon the altar atop the wood. As Isaac lay obediently and submissive upon the altar, Abraham took his knife and stood over his son. Abraham stretched forth his hand with every intention to plunge the knife swiftly and deeply into his promised son. This was the most difficult command he had ever been called on to obey, but Abraham loved and trusted his Lord. In the mind of Abraham, because of his strong love for and obedience to his Lord, Isaac's sure death was about to happen.

Abraham's hand was stretched forth, but before the knife could be plunged into Isaac, God stayed the hand of Abraham! The Lord called forth and commanded Abraham "lay not thine hand upon the lad, neither do thou any thing unto him: for now I know that thou fearest God, seeing thou hast not withheld thy son, thine only son from me"

(Genesis 22:12). At this time, Abraham looked and saw a ram caught in the thickets. This was 'Abraham's Lamb'! Oh, the joy and relief that filled Abraham's heart! He did not have to experience the terrible ordeal of sacrificing his beloved son, although he was willing to do so in obedience to, and love for, his Lord. Can you imagine the wave of thanksgiving that came over Isaac as he was spared the painful agony of being sacrificed? Though being willing to do so out of obedience to, and with a heart full of love, for his father, Isaac had been willing to be the sacrificial lamb. Thankfully, Isaac was unbound and released. Father and son joyfully embraced as they heard God's acknowledgement of their faithfulness. Isaac had been set free, for now there was a substitute found for him. The ram was placed upon the altar in Isaac's stead and sacrificed as an offering to the Lord. God indeed provided a sacrifice for the burnt offering. Abraham gave the place a fitting name: Jehovah-jireh, 'the Lord will provide'!

MacDonald makes this observation:

> There are two outstanding symbols of Christ in this chapter. Isaac is the first: an **only son**, loved by his father, willing to do his father's will, received back from the dead in a figure. The **ram** is the second: an innocent victim died as a substitute for another, its blood was shed, and it was a burnt offering wholly consumed for God. Someone has said that, in providing the **ram** as a substitute for Isaac, "God spared Abraham's heart a pang He would not spare His own."[21]

As Abraham had prophesied, he and Isaac, *both*, returned down the mountain. They had gone up the mountain together and now together they came down. Both were filled with awe and worship to the God they served. Their God was a faithful God! Joyfully, they reunited with their two young companions who had waited patiently at the campsite. One

---

[21] William MacDonald, *Believer's Bible Commentary* (Nashville, Tennessee: Thomas Nelson Publishers, 1985, 1995), 59.

wonders at the conversation that may have commenced. Did Abraham share the heart wrenching pain of his journey? Did he understand the ramifications of the experience? Did he use this opportunity to teach his companions the deep spiritual truths of God's grace and love? Unfortunately, the Bible does not reveal the answers to these questions. However, there must have been some very interesting discussions as both Abraham and Isaac gave witness to the events as they understood them.

According to Scripture, Abraham possibly understood more than one might expect concerning the ramifications of the event that had just transpired. He may have understood this to be a foreshadow of what was to come. In Galatians 3:8 one reads, "that God … preached the gospel unto Abraham … " This can be understood when the comparisons are made. Abraham offered his only begotten son as sacrifice. Although God stayed Abraham's hand from actually killing Isaac, God counted him to have carried it through," … because thou hast obeyed my voice" (Genesis 22:18b). God had provided the sacrificial ram; the 'Lamb' would be provided later. It was on the third day that Abraham figuratively received Isaac from the dead. This is a beautiful prophetic picture of the death and resurrection of Christ. This is the gospel!

There are numerous truths to be gleaned from the account of Abraham and Isaac. Regarding Abraham's obedience to God concerning Isaac, these observations are made: "Faith obeys completely and emphatically God's Word; faith surrenders the best to God holding nothing back; and faith waits on the Lord to provided for all needs."[22]

The death and blood of Isaac could not suffice as payment for sin, for he himself was a sinner, in need of a Savior. The New Testament would later provide the enlightenment that no one is without sin. Therefore, regardless of how badly someone would want to, no one could be an acceptable substitute: "For all have sinned, and come short of the glory of God" (Romans 3:23). The only way man could be redeemed would be for a sinless and purely innocent 'Man' to offer Himself as a substitute for others. Thus, the need for the God-Man, the 'Lamb of God'!

---

[22] Fruchtenbaum, *The Book of Genesis*, 358.

However, Isaac was a foreshadow of the only sinless and purely innocent sacrifice. Although God provided a ram for Abraham and not a lamb, the 'Lamb' would be provided some nineteen centuries later. Only the blood of the 'Lamb of God' could be the acceptable substitute that would propitiate the righteous wrath of God. And God provided Himself a Lamb for the sacrifice and full payment for the sin of man! That is God's love and grace in action! A major difference between Abraham's sacrifice and God's is: God did not stay His own hand, but followed through with the sacrifice of His own Son. In Romans 8:32a one reads, "He that spared not his own Son, but delivered him up for us all … " This is summarized in John the Baptist's introduction to Messiah, "Behold, the Lamb of God which taketh away the sin of the world" (John 1:29).

Before the saga is continued, let us review the parallels between Isaac and the Messiah:

1) Isaac was born by the power of God's Spirit, Galatians 4:29; Messiah was born by the power of God's Spirit; Luke 1:31, 34-35.

2) Isaac was the son of promise, Hebrews 11:17, Galatians 4:23; Messiah was the Son of many promises, Genesis 3:15, Micah 5:2.

3) Through Isaac, Abraham's descendants, God's chosen people would be identified, Hebrews 11:18; Through faith in Messiah, people are identified as the true chosen people of God, John 1:12.

4) Isaac carried the wood upon which he would be sacrificed, Genesis 22:6; Messiah would carry the 'wood' upon which He would be sacrificed, John 19:17.

5) Isaac submitted himself to his father's will, Genesis 22:9; Messiah submitted Himself to His father's will, Philippians 2:8.

6) Abraham offered his beloved son, Isaac, Genesis 22:2, 9; God would offer His beloved Son, John 3:16.

7) Isaac was offered on Mt. Moriah, Genesis 22:2; Messiah would be sacrificed on Mt. Moriah, 2 Chronicles 3:1, John 19:17.

8) Abraham was stopped by an angel of God from sacrificing Isaac, Genesis 22:11-12; An angel strengthened Messiah before His sacrifice; however, nothing could stop God from offering Messiah as a sacrifice, Matthew 26:53-54, Romans 8:32.

9) God provided a ram in substitution of Isaac, Genesis 22:13; God provided Messiah Himself as the Lamb of God as our substitute, 1 Peter 1:18-19.

10) Abraham, for three days considered his son Isaac as dead, Genesis 22:3-5; Messiah was three days and nights in the grave, Matthew 12:40.

11) Isaac was figuratively resurrected from the dead, Hebrews 11:19; Messiah was literally and physically raised from the dead, Luke 24:33-34, 1 Corinthians 15:3-4.

The Genesis account of Scripture reveals that Abraham continued his walk of faith in God and God honored the covenant He made with Abraham. When Isaac was forty years old, he married a beautiful lady, Rebekah. When Isaac was sixty years of age, Rebekah gave birth to their twin sons, Esau and Jacob. It was Jacob who became heir of the covenant promises and was blessed with twelve sons from whom the Hebrew nation would evolve.

One of the sons of Jacob, Joseph, is the main character in the latter chapters of the Book of Genesis. God began working in Joseph's life at a very early age. Joseph's brothers, motivated by jealousy, sold Joseph into slavery and feigned his death to his father, Jacob. However, God did not forsake Joseph, but turned this bad situation into good. Through a series of events, Joseph was eventually released from prison and entered the palace. God providentially established Joseph as Prime Minister of Egypt, second in command to Pharaoh. In this position, Joseph had the capability to preserve the lives of Jacob and his progeny through a severe seven year famine. This resulted in Jacob and his family moving from Canaan to Egypt. "And all the souls that came out of the loins of Jacob were seventy souls: for Joseph was in Egypt already" (Exodus 1:5). Over the next approximately one hundred years, the Hebrew people had enjoyed a secure and prosperous life that Egypt afforded. "And the children of Israel were fruitful, and increased abundantly, and multiplied, and waxed exceeding mighty; and the land was filled with them" (Exodus 1:7). It has been estimated there were now over two million Hebrews, descendants of Abraham, living in Egypt. It seems the LORD would use Egypt as an incubator as the young Hebrew nation grew. They would be protected from other hostile nations by the most powerful nation of the world at that time. However, things changed! God had prophesied to Abraham in Genesis 15:13 that his descendants would be strangers in a land that was not theirs, Egypt, and they would serve the Egyptians and be afflicted by them for four hundred years. What followed set the stage for the next foreshadow of the Lamb!

CHAPTER THREE

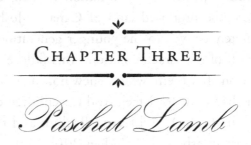

Paschal Lamb

The saga continues through Scripture into the Book of Exodus which describes the prosperity of Abraham's and Jacob's descendents, now referred to as the children of Israel, or the Hebrews. At this junction of the journey, the third foreshadow of the Lamb, the 'Paschal (Passover) Lamb' will be discovered. Before examining this foreshadow, one must make careful observation of the context of events which lead to this foreshadow. Very quickly, two very important men are introduced, Pharaoh of Egypt and Moses, the Hebrew. It is important to understand their lives and the key roles each have in the development of the children of Israel and to the 'Paschal Lamb'.

Seventy people, Jacob and his family, entered Egypt, Genesis 46:7, and within several generations the Hebrew population had multiplied to approximately two million! Scripture describes Israel's population explosion as, "And the children of Israel were fruitful, and increased abundantly, and multiplied, and waxed exceeding mighty; and the land was filled with them" (Exodus 1:7). Life seemed to be good for the children of Israel. The Israelites seemed to have grown comfortable with their *citizenship* in Egypt. In the course of time, Jacob, Joseph, his brothers, and the Pharaoh who promoted Joseph, as we learned in the previous chapter, had died.

However, Egypt was not the land God had promised to Abraham and his descendants. As now, it was the responsibility of the older generation to teach the younger generation their heritage. There is a danger of disaster which looms over the civilization that fails to accomplish this important task. The Scripture warns of such a disaster a few decades later within the Jewish nation after the death of Joshua, their leader, into the promised land of Canaan. Joshua's generation failed to adequately convey to the younger generation how God had worked on behalf of the Israelite nation. This failure resulted in " … another generation after them, which knew not the LORD, nor yet the works which he had done for Israel. And the children of Israel did evil in the sight of the LORD, and served Baalim: and they forsook the LORD God of their fathers … " (Judges 2:10b-12a).

Scripture, Exodus 1:8, introduces a Pharaoh who began to reign who had not known Joseph or the benefits of his service to the populace of Egypt. Scholars have identified this Pharaoh to have been either of three possible Egyptian Pharaohs: Ahmose I (ca. 1570-1546); Amenhotep I (ca. 1546-1525); or Thutmose (ca. 1525-1512).[23] When this new Pharaoh began to reign, things took a negative turn and the Egyptian's attitude toward the foreign Hebrews began to change. From the neighborhood to the palace, suspicion and fear of the Hebrews began to spread throughout the Egyptian population. "The native population began to look upon Israel with narrowed eyes and growing suspicion. And as we all know too well from our world's bloody history, mounting suspicion toward a people group is only a step away from prejudice … yet another step away from persecution … and but a stone's throw from genocide."[24]

What was the source of this suspicion and prejudice? When Joseph moved Jacob and his family from Canaan to Egypt, they were shepherds by trade. Joseph had instructed his father and brothers to affirm to Pharaoh their trade as being keeper's of cattle, a generic title, Genesis 46:31-34. Why? Because the Egyptians loathed shepherds and they were considered an abomination to the Egyptians! An exception was made, however, and these shepherds were accepted because they were of the

---

[23] Charles Ryrie, *Ryrie Study Bible, King James Version*. 91. Notes on Exodus 1:8.

[24] Charles Swindoll, *Moses: A Man of Selfless Dedication* (Nashville, Tennessee: W Publishing Group, a Division of Thomas Nelson, Inc., 1999), 5.

family of Joseph. Why? Because Joseph was responsible for saving Egypt during the seven years of famine and an Egyptian hero!

Unfortunately, as time passed, Joseph and those who had known him had died. The new Pharaoh, who did not know Joseph or his contributions to the welfare of Egypt, now took the throne of Egypt. This Pharaoh began to grow uneasy of the massive population of this Hebrew sheep herding community. The fear of being overrun by this foreign populace of Hebrews motivated Pharaoh to change the status of the Israelites from invited guests to captured slaves. In captivity, the Hebrews endured extreme hardships and were forced to build the treasure cities of Pithom and Raamses for Pharaoh, Exodus 1:11. Pharaoh's calculated scheme backfired! What was intended to assist in decreasing the Hebrew population had the opposite results. "But the more they afflicted them, the more they multiplied and grew" (Exodus 1:12a). Centuries earlier, the Lord had spoken to Abraham and unveiled a prophecy concerning his descendents. "And he said unto Abram, Know of a surety that thy seed shall be a stranger in a land that is not theirs, and shall serve them; and they shall afflict them four hundred years; and also that nation, whom they shall serve, will I judge; and afterward they shall come out with great substance" (Genesis 15:13-14). The affliction of His people did not take God by surprise. He knew what was coming and knew how it would end!

Pharaoh appointed taskmasters over the children of Israel. They, who were now enslaved, were rigorously afflicted by their taskmasters. The children of Israel were forced to make their own bricks, make their own mortar, were forced to work in the fields, and serve in other manners. Life for the Hebrew people had become bitter and difficult. Their hard labor was intended as a means to slow down the population explosion within the Hebrew race, but this tactic did not accomplish the desired effect. Therefore, Pharaoh devised another heartless and diabolical plan against the descendants of Abraham.

The plan this heartless Pharaoh concocted involved the Egyptian midwives. It involved infanticide! Midwives were women who assisted pregnant women as they gave birth. The Scripture introduces two women, Shiphrah and Puah, Exodus 1:15, who apparently were overseers

41

of the midwives. Shiphrah and Puah were summoned into Pharaoh's presence and given an explicit command. When the time came for the midwives to perform their duties among the Hebrew women, the midwives were to kill all the male babies, but save the lives of the female babies. "And he said, When ye do the office of a midwife to the Hebrew women, and see them upon the stools; if it be a son, then ye shall kill him: but if it be a daughter, then she shall live" (Exodus 1:16). Though the Bible commands one to obey the law, there are limits to submitting to civil authority. When man's law becomes contrary to God's law, then one should always obey God!

Though Pharaoh intended to intimidate these midwives into carrying out his heinous plan, he failed. "But the midwives feared God, and did not as the king of Egypt commanded them, but saved the men children alive" (Exodus 1:17). When Shiphrah and Puah were questioned why Pharaoh's orders were not being carried out, they replied that the Hebrew women had given birth before they had arrived on the scene. Although God did not and does not commend lying, God did bless these women for their piety and for helping His people, the children of Israel. The important role these midwives played in the preservation of the Hebrew people made them heroines to the Israelites! God honored His covenant promise he had made to Abraham, "And I will bless them that bless thee, and curse him that curseth thee" (Genesis 12:3).

Pharaoh's plan had been foiled! His persecution did not desist, but intensified. By this time, Pharaoh was fueled by enormous hatred for the Hebrews; yet, greatly feared them. He charged the entire population of Egyptians to cast all newborn males into the Nile River, Exodus 1:22. This edict set neighbor against neighbor. It was possible that when a Hebrew couple was discovered to have a newborn male child, they would be reported to the Egyptian authorities and the child would be taken into custody and thrown into the Nile to his death. Cruelty breeds cruelty!

God always has His witness in the midst of hatred and unrighteousness. Scripture introduces a Hebrew couple, Amram and Jochebed, Exodus 2:1-2; 6:20, who had a son, Moses. This son was hidden for three months. The writer of the biblical book of Hebrews reveals, "By faith Moses, when he was born, was hid three months of his parents, because they saw he was a proper child; and they were not afraid of the kings commandment" (Hebrews 11:23). Herein is the introduction to Moses, a Jew born in a place and time ruled by an anti-Semitic, tyrannical ruler. Moses' godly parents hid him for three months in spite of the peril.

After three months, it became difficult for Amram and Jochebed to hide the existence of their young son. Scripture reveals Jochebed had faith in God and she had a plan! Undoubtedly, Jochebed had done her own surveillance concerning the habit and practices of Pharaoh's daughter. Jochebed apparently had discovered that the Princess came to the river Nile to bathe at a certain time and at a particular place. Moses' mother constructed a small waterproof ark, placed young Moses into the ark, and set him afloat among the reeds at the banks of the river Nile. "Jochebed laid the ark in the flags by the river's brink, but first she laid it on the heart of God."[25] Possibly, it was at the bathing place of the Princess that the small ark was placed, in hopes the Princess would discover the child. Certainly, Moses' mother prayed that upon seeing the small baby and hearing his cry, the Princess' motherly instinct would be moved with compassion toward the child and she would spare his life. The next part of Jochebed's plan was to have Moses' older sister, Miriam, to hide and stand watch as the events of Moses' fate unfolded.

On the appointed day, Miriam hid herself, watching over the small floating bassinet containing her young brother and watching as the Princess and her maidens approached the river. Pharaoh's daughter spied the floating basket and had her servant to retrieve it. Upon opening the ark, the heart of the Princess was filled with compassion as the young baby cried. The Princess immediately recognized the child was one of the Hebrew children. Instead of obeying the edict of her father and quickly drowning the child, the Princess chose to spare the child's life. At this time, Miriam may have nonchalantly stepped out of her hiding

---

[25] D. L. Moody, *Notes from My Bible and One thousand and One Thoughts from My Library* (Grand Rapids, Michigan: Baker Book House, Reprinted August 1979), 28.

place and asked permission from the Princess to allow her to assist in finding a suitable nurse for the child. Upon receiving permission, Miriam left to recruit Jochebed (unbeknown to the Princess to be the young child's mother) to care for the newly found babe!

God is so good! God honored the faith of Moses' parents. What a blessing! The LORD answered Jochebed's apparent prayer and gave far more than she had asked for! He granted her son back into her care, she now had the protection for her son's life by the Pharaoh himself, and she, as a slave, was going to be compensated to keep and raise her own child! Wow, what a mighty and awesome God!

Scripture veils the length of time and the events which transpired during Moses' young life. He apparently remained in the care of his parents through his formative, preschool years. During this time, it seems apparent that Moses was taught about the LORD and his Hebrew heritage. Moses witnessed the faith of his parents. Possibly, he was repeatedly told the story of how his life had come to be spared. At the appointed time, Moses was brought to Pharaoh's daughter to become her son. "And the child grew, and she brought him to Pharaoh's daughter, and he became her son. And she called his name Moses: and she said, Because I drew him out of the water" (Exodus 2:10). Interestingly, Scripture does not reveal the name given to him by his parents, Amram and Jochebed.

What a change in the life of young Moses! He moved from the security and comfort of his family and the small home of a slave to the unfamiliar and overwhelming amenities of the palace and became the Prince of Egypt! Moses left a family that worshipped the one true God and entered an environment of idolatry, for the Egyptians were known for their polytheism. The years following Moses' adoption into Pharaoh's family, he became a recipient of the finest education available in Egypt.

Egypt was known for its great knowledge of astronomy, chemistry, and science. Egypt was also home to one of the largest libraries of the known world. As a member of the royal family and potential heir to the throne, Moses surely was schooled in diplomacy and became mightily skilled in warfare. Certainly, he was instructed in Egypt's religion and the worship of their various gods. All of Egypt's power, prestige, and prominence was bestowed upon Moses, the Hebrew. There was nothing withheld! According to Scripture, "Moses was learned in all the wisdom of the Egyptians and was mighty in words and in deeds" (Acts 7:22). "The amazing irony of God's divine plan was that this one whom the princess renamed, nurtured, reared, and educated in all the ways of the Egyptians, became the instrument of judgment in the very court where he grew up."[26]

When Moses reached the age of forty, he apparently became nostalgic. Possibly, he reminisced of the time spent at his birth mother's knee and remembered all she had taught him. He specifically recalled her instruction concerning his heritage and her faith in the LORD Jehovah. (Hebrews 11:24-25 substantiates this assumption.) Moses decided to visit the Hebrew slave encampment. Scripture describes it as, " … it came into his heart to visit his brethren the children of Israel" (Acts 7:23b). As he toured the grounds, he witnessed the affliction of the Hebrews, his people. He encountered an Egyptian taskmaster beating a Hebrew. Scripture reveals Moses' deliberate actions concerning his defense of the beaten Israelite. "And he looked this way and that way, and when he saw that there was no man, he slew the Egyptian, and hid him in the sand" (Exodus 2:12). Moses looked both ways horizontally, but never looked *up* seeking God's direction. What could Moses have been thinking at this time? He was the 'Prince of Egypt' and stood to lose so much because of this action. The death penalty awaited him if his deed was discovered. Scripture enlightens us to Moses' motivation, "For he supposed his brethren would have understood how God by his hand would deliver them: but they understood not" (Acts 7:25). Apparently, God had put within the heart and mind of Moses that he would one day be instrumental in delivering Israel out of Egypt's bondage, but Moses had acted hastily and out of the will of God.

The imagination of this writer now envisions what could have prompted Moses to act as he did. Possibly, when young Moses received Jochebed's, (his mother), instruction concerning his Hebrew heritage,

---

[26] Charles Swindoll, *Moses: A Man of Selfless Dedication*, 32.

she may very well have related the account of Joseph. Jochebed may have described to Moses how Joseph had been sold into slavery in Egypt and that by the providence of Jehovah God had been promoted to second in command to Pharaoh of Egypt. Joseph was God's instrument of deliverance of Israel from seven years of famine. Moses may have thought, since he had been brought from slavery to the heir of the throne of Egypt, he was placed there providentially for the deliverance of Israel from slavery and the oppression of Egypt. Moses was in a position, it seemed, to do as he pleased. He was the 'Prince of Egypt', untouchable!

Moses was to be Israel's deliverer. Unfortunately, though Moses knew about Jehovah God, he had not been schooled in the ways of God. He only knew the ways of Egypt and thought he would deliver Israel through force and might. But, God had a better plan and it would involve the 'Paschal Lamb'! There was no mistake God would deliver the Hebrew nation from the oppression of Egypt, but He would accomplish this in a way that there would be no mistake that it was by the hand of God, not man. Moses, who was accustomed to getting what he wanted, when he wanted it, did not wait for the timing and direction of the LORD.

The next day, Moses went again to the Hebrew encampment and observed two Hebrew men arguing, Exodus 2:13-14b. Moses decided to intervene and attempted to negotiate peace between the two men. After all, they were both Israelites and should be supportive of each other. One of the men then challenged Moses and inquired if Moses intended to kill him as he had killed the Egyptian the day before. Moses became aware his murderous deed was known. "And Moses feared, and said, Surely, this thing is known. Now when Pharaoh heard this thing, he sought to slay Moses. But Moses fled from the face of Pharaoh, and dwelt in the land of Midian: and sat down by a well" (Exodus 2:14c-15).

As a result of Moses' action, he had to escape Egypt for his life. Moses went from the comforts of the royal palace to the desolate, barren, desert land of Midian. Midian was an area east of Egypt on the Sinai Peninsula, inhabited by the descendants of Abraham's nomadic sons, birthed by his latter wife, Keturah, Genesis 25:2. Moses had arrived at a point in his life where all resources had been exhausted. In the midst of this dry desert, Moses found an oasis of life and sat down by a well; a well that afforded new life to a thirsty soul.

Though Moses was a very educated man, he needed some advanced education. He was about to enter B.D.U., 'Backside of the Desert University'! The LORD Jehovah was about to school Moses in the supernatural. Moses would learn how the living God could take someone who possibly now considered himself unqualified and unusable and proceed to work extraordinary and powerful miracles through him. Swindoll quotes an observation made by D. L. Moody concerning Moses' biography, "Moses spent the first forty years of his life thinking he was somebody. He spent his second forty years learning he was a nobody. He spent his third forty years discovering what God can do with a nobody."[27]

It was in the land of Midian that Moses became acquainted with Jethro, the priest of Midian. Moses had come to the aid of Jethro's daughters when they were attacked by some shepherds as the women attempted to water their flocks. Because of the kindness shown by Moses, Jethro invited Moses to dwell at his home. Through the course of time, Moses married Zipporah, one of Jethro's daughters. Zipporah and Moses had a son to whom they gave the name of Gershom, which means 'a stranger here'. Moses knew within his heart—this was not his home!

Since Moses had fled Egypt, he had learned to survive in the desert. Now, Moses learned the occupation of a shepherd and watched over Jethro's flock. Scripture says that Moses, " … led the flock to the backside of the desert, and came to the mountain of God, even to Horeb" (Exodus 3:1b). Horeb is another name for Mount Sinai, a significant place within the history of the nation of Israel. At this time, Scripture reveals that the Pharaoh of Egypt who sought Moses' life had died, Exodus 2:23. The Hebrew people began to cry out to Jehovah God because of their slavery and oppression. "And God heard their groaning, and God remembered his covenant with Abraham, with Isaac, and with Jacob. And God looked upon the children of Israel, and

---

[27] Charles Swindoll, *Moses: A Man of Selfless Dedication*, 20.

God had respect unto them" (Exodus 2:24-25). God heard the prayers of His people and He remembered His covenant. The time had come that God would redeem Israel from the bondage and captivity of Egypt and bring Israel into the land promised to Abraham.

One day as Moses was watching over his father-in-law's sheep on Mount Sinai, Moses noticed a most peculiar sight; a bush which was burning, but not being consumed. Through this phenomenon, Moses encountered the living God! God initiated a dialogue with Moses through the burning bush, introducing Himself as the God of Abraham, Isaac, and Jacob. Jehovah God brings Moses' attention, first and foremost, to the holiness of God by commanding Moses to remove his shoes, for he was standing on holy ground, Exodus 3:5-6. This divine manifestation of God, (theophany), struck fear into Moses and he hid his face, refusing to look upon Holy God!

In one's life, relation with God, and one's interaction with the LORD, one needs to recognize that God is holy! God calls and commands each individual throughout Scripture to 'be holy, for I am holy'. It is imperative that one recognizes God's holiness! When one does, one will simultaneously recognize and acknowledge one's sinfulness and need for God's grace and forgiveness. At this time, God will be able to minister His grace and mercy and draw one to the place of acceptance into His holy presence and allow one to fellowship with Him. It is only through God's provision that one is able to enter into His holy presence. When a believer understands that Holy God lives within him, then he understands that everywhere he stands is holy ground! One's behavior will reflect that belief. God's people today have lost sight of this important truth and attribute of our Lord. God desires His people to be holy and conduct themselves as holy!

The LORD revealed His name, *Yahweh*, to Moses, which means "I AM THAT I AM" (Exodus 3:14). Ryrie indicates the name *Yahweh* carries the inner meaning of "I am the One who is", emphasizing God's dynamic and active self-existence.[28]

---

[28] Charles Ryrie, *Ryrie Study Bible, King James Version*, 94. Notes on Exodus 3:14.

The LORD said to Moses, "I am come down to deliver them out of the hand of the Egyptians … " (Exodus 3:8a). God informed Moses that he would be the man through whom He would confront Pharaoh to bring about the deliverance of His people, leading them back to Mount Sinai to serve the one true living God, Exodus 3:10-12. The LORD also commissioned Aaron, Moses' elder brother, to accompany him in this endeavor, Exodus 4:14. God is a personal God! He hears, He remembers, He redeems.

After forty years in the land of Midian, Moses had become a different person. He remembered the last incident in Egypt when he initiated a feeble and futile attempt to deliver the Hebrews from slavery. His hasty action resulted in the murder of an Egyptian and an unsuccessful attempt to conceal his crime. The Hebrew people resented Moses' assumption of superiority due to his position. Moses assumed the Israelites would readily accept him as their deliverer. However, they rejected Moses' assertion of self-appointed deliverer and rebelled against him. A lesson for all to learn from the actions of Moses: "When God is in it … it flows. When the flesh is in it … it's forced."[29]

Moses was now a man of humility, reluctance, and uncertainty. Instead of being prideful, confident, and deliberate, he was stripped of all self-confidence. Moses was no longer "one mighty in words and deeds" (Acts 7:22b). Moses was now doubtful God could, or would, use him and reluctant to attempt to deliver the Hebrews from Egypt. He would need to completely depend on God. Now, God could use Moses for the purpose for which he was called—to deliver Israel.

Scripture presents the LORD's seven 'I wills' of redemption in Exodus 6:6-8. God told Moses: *I will* bring you out from under your burdens; *I will* rid you out of your bondage; *I will* redeem you with a stretched out arm; *I will* take you to Me for a people; *I will* be to you, your God; *I will* bring you into the land I promised Abraham; *I will* give you the land for an heritage. Deliverance of Israel was a certainty; but, it would not come without resistance! The enemy of God never gives up without a fight! Satan desires to keep God's people enslaved

---

[29] Charles Swindoll, *Moses: A Man of Selfless Dedication*, 57.

and oppressed. But, God always shows Himself mighty on behalf of His people!

The Lord commissioned Moses to deliver His people in a way very different than the way Moses would have thought deliverance would be achieved. Moses was warned by God, "And I am sure that the king of Egypt will not let you go, no, not by a mighty hand" (Exodus 3:19). The LORD informed Moses that deliverance would come only through the miraculous power of God.

God's *mighty hand* would be evidenced by destructive and disastrous plagues of judgment He would bring against Egypt. Though the Egyptian Pharaoh was the principle figure Moses encountered, Scripture enlightens to the primary reason God wrought judgment upon Egypt. Exodus 12:12b reads, " … and against all the gods of Egypt I will execute judgment: I am the LORD." Egypt was a polytheistic nation. They worshipped multiple false gods. The Egyptians were immersed into idolatry. This religious worldview was destroying the souls of the Egyptian people. God desires all men to know Him, the One True God! Therefore, Almighty God declared war against these false gods!

Moses and Aaron returned to Egypt and met with the elders of Israel and related to them the events that led to Moses' reason for returning to Egypt after forty years of exile. All the Israelites excitedly worshipped the LORD at the news that God was about to deliver them from slavery and the oppression of Egypt. Remember: 'When God is in it, it flows'. However, none realized it would not be a quick, or easy, deliverance.

When Moses and Aaron met with Pharaoh and delivered God's message to him, they did not receive the same reception as with the Israelites. God's message was for Pharaoh to release the Israelites, God's people, and free them to worship Him on the mountain of God, Exodus 5:1. Pharaoh's response was defiant, adamant, and deliberate. "And Pharaoh said, Who is the LORD, that I should obey his voice to let Israel go? I know not the LORD, neither will I let Israel go" (Exodus 5:2). In Egypt's culture of the day, Pharaoh was considered a god. Therefore, Pharaoh refused to acknowledge the LORD and humble himself to God's demands.

When someone receives a clear and direct command from God and refuses to heed and obey, their heart becomes hardened, or stubborn, against the will of God. Moody observed, "If a man rejects mercy he becomes hardened. The same sun that melts the ice hardens the clay."[30] Pharaoh's denial of the One True God initiated the hardening of Pharaoh's heart toward God's mercy.

Moses and Israel were about to learn that doing the will of God always ignites the opposition of the world and Satan! The encounter between Moses and Pharaoh resulted in Pharaoh ordering more intense labor to be placed upon the Israelite slaves. A life of hardship immediately became intensely more difficult. Now the stage had been set for Jehovah God to show Himself as Redeemer of His people and to prove Himself to be the One True God to the Egyptians.

Ten plagues fell upon Egypt as the hand of God came against the various false gods of the Egyptians.[31] The first plague levied against Egypt was turning the water of the Nile River into blood, Exodus 7:14-24. Through this judgment, God proved Himself more powerful than Egypt's false gods, Hapi (spirit of the Nile) and Khnum (guardian of the Nile). Pharaoh refused to obey the command of God and hardened his heart against the voice of God.

The second judgment God wrought through Moses was calling the multitude of frogs out of the Nile to plague Egypt, Exodus 8:1-15. By this, God judged and defeated the false gods, Heqt (form of a frog) and Hapi (spirit of the Nile). Again, Pharaoh refused to obey the command of God and hardened his heart against the voice of God.

God's third judgment was probably against Egypt's priests themselves. Swarms of lice plagued Egypt, infesting all, including the false priests, who were proven powerless to deliver themselves. They were forced to acknowledge to Pharaoh that this plague was the hand of God, Exodus 8:16-19. Yet again, Pharaoh refused to obey the command of God and hardened his heart against the voice of God.

---

[30] D. L. Moody, *Notes from My Bible and One thousand and One Thoughts from My Library*, 30. Notes on Exodus 4:21.
[31] Ryrie. *Ryrie Study Bible, King James Version*. Chart on page 101.

The fourth judgment to fall upon Egypt was the plague of flies, Exodus 8:20-32. This judgment came against the false god, Uatchit (a god who manifested himself as a fly). Pharaoh continued to harden his heart toward God.

God's fifth judgment wrought through Moses was the plague of disease upon the Egyptians' cattle, Exodus 9:1-7. This plague focused on and judged the false gods of the sacred bulls and cows: Apis, Ptah, Mnrvis, and Hathor. Pharaoh continued to harden his heart to God and refused to let the people of Israel leave.

The sixth judgment involved a plague of boils and sores upon both man and beast, Exodus 9:8-12. Through this judgment, Jehovah proved Himself more powerful than the false gods, Sekhmet (goddess with power to heal) and Serapis (healing god). The magicians whom the Pharaoh relied upon were unable to stand before Pharaoh or Moses because of the boils upon themselves, which they were powerless to overcome. But once again, Pharaoh hardened his heart to God.

God's seventh judgment upon Egypt and their false gods was the destruction of the crops and cattle by means of hail, Exodus 9:13-35. By this plague, God defeated the false gods, Seth (protector of the crops) and Nut (sky goddess). This plague also touches both man and beast. Interestingly, some of the Egyptian citizens were beginning to recognize the power of the God of Moses and Israel. This is evidenced in, "He that feared the word of the LORD among the servants of Pharaoh made his servants and his cattle flee into the houses. And he that regarded not the word of the LORD left his servants and cattle in the field" (Exodus 9:20-21). Although Pharaoh feigned an acknowledgment of confession that the LORD was the righteous God, he in reality, hardened his heart even more, Exodus 9:27-28, 34-35.

The eighth judgment brought the plague of locusts to destroy the remaining Egyptians crops, Exodus 10:1-20. Egypt's false gods, Isis (goddess of life) and Seth (protector of crops) were powerless against the hand of the One True God. Pharaoh once again feigned acknowledging his sin and asking forgiveness; in return requesting that Moses rescind the plague. Once the locusts were gone, Pharaoh again hardened his heart.

God's ninth judgment focused on the false gods, Re (the sun god) and Atum (god of the setting sun). This was a plague of darkness that covered all of Egypt, except the land where the Hebrews dwelt, Exodus 10:21-29. Scripture describes this as a darkness that could be felt and lasted for three days. Still, Pharaoh hardened his heart.

The tenth and final judgment would introduce and involve the 'Paschal Lamb'. This judgment, the most horrific of all the judgments, comes against the false god, Osiris (giver of life) and Pharaoh who was considered deity, Exodus 11:1-12:36. Through Moses, God warned Pharaoh one last time to let His people go or He would send death to the land by the killing of the firstborn of every family. Each home that did not fear and obey God would experience this horrific tragedy. Though Israel's redemption was close at hand, they would not automatically be exempt from this last plague. But, God tempered His judgment on Egypt with mercy and perfect provision—the substitution of a life for a life!

God told Moses to instruct the people to take one lamb per household and to slaughter it at twilight. According to the historian, Josephus, it was customary to slaughter the lamb at approximately three o'clock in the afternoon. The lamb's blood was to be applied to the top and sides of the doorframe of the entry door to the home. Though these instructions may not have been the most sensible to Moses, the Bible says of Moses, "Through faith he kept the passover, and the sprinkling of blood, lest he that destroyed the firstborn touch them" (Hebrews 11:28). Obedience to these instructions would provide protection for all in the home. Upon seeing the blood, the plague of death would not enter the home, but would pass over it; thus, the 'Passover'. God emphasized the importance of the application of the shed blood: "And the blood shall be to you for a token upon the houses where ye are: and when I see the blood, I will pass over you, and the plague shall not be upon you to destroy you, when I smite the land of Egypt" (Exodus 12:13).

The LORD balances His righteousness with mercy. This was a night of judgment, but the substitionary death of the Passover Lamb, the 'Paschal Lamb', *provided* covering, or atonement, for God's people and *protected* them from the wrath of the Almighty. The Passover and 'Paschal Lamb' provided tremendous object lessons. Moses instructed the people that the lamb had to be the best of the flock and this chosen lamb was marked for death. After sacrificing this lamb and applying its blood as instructed, it was to be roasted with fire without the breaking of any bone, and was to consumed with bitter herbs and unleavened bread by the entire household.

This innocent 'Paschal Lamb' would foreshadow the One who would come centuries later to become God's final means of atonement and redemption. Take notice of these the parallels between the 'Paschal Lamb' and the 'Lamb of God':

1) Applying the blood upon the top and sides of the front door made a sign of a bloody cross. Centuries later, the 'Lamb of God' would shed His blood upon a cross, Colossians 1:20.

2) The blood of the 'Paschal Lamb' set apart the homes of those who believed and obeyed God from those who did not. Those who apply, in faith, the blood of the 'Lamb of God' to the door of their hearts, God sets them apart as His children, John 1:12.

3) When the people entered through the blood stained door that first Passover, they found safety from the wrath of God. Scripture gives assurance concerning one's trust in the 'Lamb of God' that, "Much more then, being now justified by his blood, we shall be saved from wrath through him" (Romans 5:9).

4) The roasting of the 'Paschal Lamb' with fire was symbolic of the lamb bearing God's judgment in our stead. The prophesied 'Lamb of God' would be " … delivered for our offences … " (Romans 4:25), and would deliver those who trust in His blood sacrifice from the wrath to come, 1 Thessalonians 1:10.

5) 5) The bitter herbs were synonymous with mourning and were to remind the people their firstborn lived because the 'Paschal Lamb' died. Scripture speaks of the 'Lamb of God', "Who died for us, that … we should live together with him" (1 Thessalonians 5:10).

The dawn of the next morning revealed much grief and sorrow among those who did not believe the warning, for death had visited their homes. This included Pharaoh's home and firstborn child. Though Pharaoh was worshipped as deity, he could not escape and had fallen defenseless against the power of the One True God! Fearful now of the true God of Israel, the Egyptians forced the Israelites to leave their nation, encouraging them to depart with all their possessions, plus great treasures, Exodus 12:33-36. This wealth, some scholars believe, was simply back wages the Egyptians owed to the Hebrews for four hundred years of slave labor! The night before, the Hebrews were a timid, enslaved people, eating their meal behind closed doors. This day the sun rose upon a free nation, some two million strong, enroute to a land God had promised their forefathers centuries before. "And also that nation, whom they shall serve, will I judge: and afterward they shall come out with great substance" (Genesis 15:14).

The night of the LORD's Passover had such important significance that Moses was instructed to make this a memorial for the entire nation of Israel to remember when and how God had delivered Israel from the slavery of Egypt. "And this day shall be unto you for a memorial; and ye shall keep it a feast to the LORD throughout your generations; ye shall keep it a feast by an ordinance for ever" (Exodus 12:14).

Egypt, blinded by the enemy of God, Satan, and led into idol worship had learned the LORD is greater than all other gods. The Israelites had been enslaved to an idolatrous nation for over four hundred years. God had shown Israel that He was superior and was the One True God. Motivated by divine love and grace, the LORD had delivered His people from the captivity and oppression of the 'enemy' through the 'blood of the lamb'.

Moses began leading the massive population of Hebrews out of Egypt toward the land of Canaan. Throughout this eventful journey, they encountered multiple setbacks and obstacles. In each instance, God proved Himself faithful to His people. Repeatedly, Jehovah manifested His great power and ability to protect and provide for His people. God began with parting the waters of the mighty Red Sea, allowing the Israelites to cross over on dry ground. His protective hand delivered the Israelites from assailing armies. As this vast multitude of Hebrews traveled through the desert the next forty years, God faithfully supplied daily provisions of manna and quail. He miraculously supplied water from rocks and kept their clothes and sandals from deteriorating.

One of the landmarks of the journey of the Israelites took place at Mount Sinai. This is the place where God had first revealed Himself to Moses in the burning bush and promised Moses that he would return there years later to serve Him. The Scripture reveals God speaking to Moses, "And he said, Certainly I will be with thee; and this shall be a token unto thee, that I have sent thee: When thou hast brought forth the people out of Egypt, ye shall serve God upon this mountain" (Exodus 3:12). At the top of this mountain, God manifested Himself to the Israelites in the form of smoke, fire, lightning, and thunder. From the top of Mount Sinai, God spoke to Moses in the cloud of His glory. Moses received the commandments of God, written by the finger of God on stone tablets. God also instructed Moses in the construction of the tent of the Tabernacle and its instruments of worship. The people of God would reverence this Tabernacle, for this is where God would meet with and speak to men.

God moved from the mountain top into the Tabernacle upon its completion. The final chapter of the Book of Exodus describes the astounding event. "Then the cloud covered the tent of the congregation, and the glory of the LORD filled the tabernacle. And Moses was not able to enter the tent of the congregation, because the cloud abode thereon, and the glory of the LORD filled the tabernacle" (Exodus 40:34-35). Out of the Tabernacle, God instructed Moses concerning five sacrifices through which the Israelites would worship Jehovah, Leviticus 1:1. The instructions included the manner and elements of sacrifice. Each individual sacrifice would provide a particular aspect of the prophesied Messiah. When connected together, the next foreshadow, the 'Levitical Lamb', is revealed. The minute pictures combined provide a more comprehensive look at the supreme sacrifice—the 'Lamb of God.'

The journey continues into Leviticus, a biblical book most people avoid. Yet, it reveals a look at the 'Levitical Lamb'; the Person and work of the Redeemer.

CHAPTER FOUR

Levitical Lamb

The journey continues through the Holy Scriptures in search for the next foreshadow. The road leads one on what many consider a burdensome trek. Many have refused to walk down this stretch of road, fearful of being overwhelmed or bored with legalistic terminology. Surprisingly, within the Book of Leviticus, an important portrait of the Person and work of the promised Redeemer of man is presented.

The foreshadow of the 'Levitical Lamb' will not focus as much on a literal sacrifice, as it will on the requirements the LORD prescribed for an acceptable sacrifice. Within the first seven chapters of the Book of Leviticus are instructions and ordinances given pertaining to five sacrifices for the nation of Israel. The 1) burnt offering, 2) meat (also called grain) offering, and 3) peace offering were voluntary offerings and they provide one with a picture of the *Person* of the Redeemer. The compulsory offerings were the 4) sin offering and the 5) trespass offering and they provide one with a picture of the *work* of the Redeemer. Within the New Testament, the four gospels present the earthly life of the Messiah. Likewise, in the Book of Leviticus, the five offerings present the prophesied Messiah's (Lamb of God) Person and work. These sacrifices culminate on the annual observation of the Day of Atonement, Leviticus 16, which is the foreshadow of the redemptive work of the 'Lamb of God'. As one studies theses various sacrifices, one will begin to unfold the 'mystery of the gospel' contained within the Old Testament and brought to fulfillment in the New Testament.

The Book of Exodus concludes with Moses completing the construction of the Tabernacle. God came down from the top of Mount Sinai where He had been meeting Moses and He filled the tabernacle with. "Then a cloud covered the tent of the congregation, and the glory of the LORD filled the tabernacle" (Exodus 40:34). It is out of the tabernacle that God speaks to Moses, Leviticus 1:1, and begins to provide the ordinances and instructions pertaining to properly acceptable sacrifices.

Moses was told to instruct the children of Israel that the offering brought to the LORD was to be from their herd (cattle) or their flock (sheep). This indicates a domesticated and peaceable animal, not one taken from the wild. The individual's chosen offering was to be the best of their possession, dear to them, and costly to them. Anyone could bring an offering to the LORD as indicated by Leviticus 1:2b, "If *any* man ... " (Leviticus 1:3b, italics mine) and this would be a voluntary offering.

The burnt offering is the oldest offering known to man and was the offering presented by Abel, Noah, and Abraham. Those who desired to approach God would present a burnt offering. The Hebrew word for this burnt sacrifice, *olah*, means "that which ascends." All of the animal, except the blood, was completely consumed in the fire and 'ascended' up in smoke. This offering symbolized the voluntary and complete devotion and consecration of the one offering the sacrifice to God. This same presentation of complete dedication to God is pictured in the life of a New Testament Christian. The Scripture encourages one to " ... present your bodies a living sacrifice unto God, which is your reasonable service" (Romans 12:1b).

Interestingly, the burnt offering could be either a bull, a male sheep or goat, a male or female dove, or a male or female pigeon. The sacrifice was to be the best that an individual could offer. This animal had to be without blemish and without any defect. This pictures the sinless perfection of the coming Redeemer of whom Scripture says, " ... who is holy, harmless, undefiled, separate from sinners ... " (Hebrews 7:26);

and "In Him is no sin" (1 John 3:5). A lame, sickly, or unwanted animal would not be accepted. It had to be ideally perfect. Provisions were made for all classes of people to offer sacrifice to God. The prominent and affluent would offer a bull. The most impoverished individual would offer a dove, or pigeon. This allowed any, and everyone, to offer sacrifice to God. No one was excluded! A worthy note to consider is found in the lives of Joseph and Mary, as they indicated their poverty by presenting an offering of two doves, Luke 2:24.

When presenting the sacrifice, the animal would be brought to the altar. The offerer would publicly place his hands upon the animal, symbolizing the animal's substitution for the offerer. The offerer himself would then kill the animal. Metaphorically, the sins of the offerer killed the animal which was being offered as his substitute. Dr. McGee shares an excerpt from Dr. Kellogg concerning the laying on of the hands. "It symbolized a transfer, according to God's merciful provision, of an obligation to suffer for sin, from the offerer to the innocent victim. Henceforth, the victim stood in the offerer's place, and was dealt with accordingly."[32]

After the slaying of the sacrifice, the priests would take the blood of the sacrifice and sprinkle it around the altar. If the sacrifice was a bull, sheep, or a goat, the animal would be cut into pieces. A bull would also be flayed (skinned). The head and fat would be placed upon the burning altar, representing the best of the animal. The animal's inwards and legs would be thoroughly washed in water; that which was presented to God must be clean. The meat was then salted, Ezekiel 43:24, and placed upon the altar to be consumed. Thrice, the Scriptures declare the burnt offering, " ... a sweet savour unto the LORD" (Leviticus 1:9b, 13c, 17c), indicating God's satisfaction and acceptance of the sacrifice. If the sacrifice was a pigeon or a dove, the priest would pluck the feathers from the fowls and burn them upon the altar.

The burnt offering presents the whole and complete dedication of the Redeemer as man's substitute to God. The offering of the various

---

[32] J. Vernon McGee, *Thru The Bible, Vol. 1* (Nashville, Tennessee: Thomas Nelson Publishers, 1981), 327.

animals speaks of the Person and value of the death of Christ, in expressions of His devotion to the will of His Father. The bull typifies devoted service; the sheep typifies devoted submission; the goat typifies sin-bearing; and the doves and pigeons typify devoted sacrifice.[33] It was Christ who, "hath given himself for us an offering and a sacrifice to God for a sweetsmelling savor" (Ephesians 5:2).

The meat (grain or meal) offering was the only bloodless sacrifice to be offered. It was a voluntary expression of thanksgiving and praise to the LORD. This sacrifice always accompanied the burnt offering; but sometimes was offered alone. Scripture describes this offering in Leviticus 2:1-16 and 6:14-23. It is important to examine the ingredients which were included and those excluded with this offering.

Included in the grain offering were fine flour, oil, frankincense, and salt. All these ingredients combined constituted the grain offering. This offering foreshadowed the perfect humanity of the Messiah and the value of His death. These ingredients were combined to be baked into a cake, or bread. The fine flour pictured the evenness and well integrated personality and the moral perfection of the Messiah. He was the only one who could totally hate sin and evil, but at the same time unconditionally love the sinner!

The oil was to be poured upon the fine flour, Leviticus 2:1; it was to be mingled with the fine flour, verse 4; the oil was to be poured thereon, verse 6; the offering was to presented with oil, verse 7. The grain offering was to be saturated with the oil. This signified the Holy Spirit who was prominent in the perfect, holy, earthly life of the Messiah. He was 'born of the Spirit', Luke 1:35; He was 'baptized with the Spirit', Matthew 3:16-17; He was 'led by the Spirit', Mark 1:12; and His teaching, miracles, and the offering of Himself was 'by the Spirit', Matthew 12:28; John 3:34; and Acts 10:38.

Frankincense was a form of incense mixed with various spices, Exodus 30:34. This incense would only exude its fragrance when it was crushed, beaten, burned, or placed under pressure. The graciousness and

---

[33] Stephen F. Olford, *The Tabernacle: Camping with God* (Grand Rapids, Michigan: Kregel Publications, 1971, 2004), 140.

sweetness of the Messiah was observed by all in His presence when He came under pressure from the religious leaders as they, " … wondered at the gracious words which proceeded out of his mouth" (Luke 4:22). When the Messiah was beaten and crucified He prayed, "Father forgive them; for they know not what they do" (Luke 23:34).

The salt was incorporated into the offering as a preservative. It is referred to as the 'salt of the covenant' in Leviticus 2:13. This typified the faithfulness of the Messiah. He is called the " … Faithful and True" (Revelation 19:11).

The ingredients specifically forbidden in the grain offering were leaven and honey, Leviticus 2:11. Throughout Scripture, leaven is representative of evil and sin. Honey, though initially sweet, would ferment and sour. Within the earthly life of the Messiah, there was no sin, evil, or corruptness. He knew no sin and was without spot or blemish, 1 John 3:5; 1 Peter 1:19.

A portion of the grain offering was to be offered unto the LORD by fire and received as a "sweet savour unto the LORD" (Leviticus 2:9). The remainder of the grain offering belonged to the priests, Leviticus 2:9-10. Therefore, this offering presents the fragrant loveliness and perfectness of the human persona of the Messiah. The Messiah is to be received by faith and His life is to be imparted to the recipient. He is the 'Bread of Life', John 6:48. Hallelujah! He was, is, and always shall be the perfect Savior!

The peace offering, Leviticus 3, was always presented in conjunction with the burnt offering. This was another voluntary offering and emphasized the communion and fellowship of believers with God through the Messiah.

The peace offering would come from either the herd or the flock. The instructions were again explicit to ensure the animal was without blemish. As the animal was presented at the altar, the offerer would identify with the sacrifice by the laying on of his hands upon its head. Then, the offerer himself would sacrifice the animal. The priests would sprinkle the blood about the altar. Only the best animals were to be offered as a sacrifice and the best of the animal belonged to God. These best portions were described within the instructions and these portions would be placed upon the altar and burned. Very clearly, the blood and the fat belonged to the LORD.

The animals to be offered as a sacrifice were either a bullock, heifer, lamb, or goat. Each of these animals presented a trait of the Person who would be man's Redeemer. The bullock, or heifer, presented the Redeemer as a servant. The lamb identified the Redeemer with man, in both life and death. The goat identified the Redeemer as adequate to take away the sin of man.

However, unlike the burnt offering, either a bullock or heifer could be offered as a peace offering; however, no fowls could be used in the peace offering. Only a specified portion of the sacrifice would be presented upon the altar. The remainder of the peace offering was shared by both priests and the offerer. This pictured fellowship between God and man, as well as between man and man. According to Leviticus 7:15, the entire portion of sacrifice that belonged to the offerer was to be eaten the same day in its entirety. Eating the offering the same day as it was offered signified that a personal fellowship with the LORD should be real and remain fresh. "In the peace offering, the emphasis is not upon the peace that He made by the blood of the cross, but upon the peace He *is* because of the blood of the cross."[34] The center of, and the basis for, the fellowship is the Person. Christ brings us together with each other and with God. "For He is our peace, who hath made both one, and hath broken down the middle wall of partition between us" (Ephesians 2:14).

The first three of the five offerings presented a picture of the Person and portrayed various traits and attributes of the Redeemer. Each of these sacrifices was commended to be a "sweet smelling savor unto the LORD". Strong emphasis was placed upon the animal having no defects and being unblemished. Because of His unblemished, spotless, and sinless life, the Redeemer would be the only acceptable and adequate sacrifice for man's sin. However, one must remember the truth McGee presents: "It is not the spotless life of Christ and our approval of Him

---

[34] J. Vernon McGee, *Thru The Bible, Vol. 1*, 333.

that saves us. Only His death can save the sinner."[35] The price of sin is death and the blood must be shed for the forgiveness of sin!

The first non-sweet savor offering was the sin offering, Leviticus 4; 6:24-30. The sin offering was the most important and significant offering of all. It was offered during each Jewish feast: Passover, Pentecost, Trumpets, and Tabernacles. Through the blood of this offering the High Priest would enter the Holy of Holies once a year on the Day of Atonement. The Holy Spirit led Moses to use more Scripture to describe and record this offering than any of the others and He regarded this offering to be of utmost importance! It was through this offering the atonement of sin was made. The sin offering clarifies the Scripture, "For the life of the flesh is in the blood: and I have given it to you upon the altar to make atonement for your souls: It is the blood that maketh atonement for the soul" (Leviticus 17:11).

Through the sin offering, one will learn that man is a sinner by nature. God instructed Moses, " ... If a soul shall sin through ignorance against any of the commandments of the LORD concerning things which ought not to be done, and shall do against any of them" (Leviticus 4:2). Man possesses an innate sin nature. He sins because he is a sinner; not a sinner because he sins. If any doubt this, one simply must observe the actions of small children. A child does not have to be taught how to lie, but taught to tell the truth. Selfishness is naturally demonstrated in a child and he must be taught how to share. These are but two examples that expose the innate sin nature. One must come to acknowledge one's sinfulness before Holy God. The Psalmist prayed, " ... cleanse me from my secret faults" (Psalm 19:12). Again in Psalm 90:8 one reads, "Thou hast set our iniquities before thee, our secret sins in the light of thy countenance."

As the offerer laid his hand upon the head of the animal to be sacrificed, a deep guilt of conviction of sin should have resulted. This conviction was essential to understand the symbolic transfer of the guilt of sin from the individual to the animal. Before true repentance can take place in the heart of an individual, conviction of sin must be

---

[35] J. Vernon McGee, *Thru The Bible, Vol. 1*, 326

birthed within the heart. The Psalmist prayed, "Search me, O God, and know my heart; try me, and know my thoughts: And see if there be any wicked way in me, and lead me in the way everlasting" (Psalm 139:23-24). David confessed, "Against thee, thee only, have I sinned ... " (Psalm 51:4). Conviction of sin must precede repentance!

This offering for sin teaches that man should begin to view himself as God sees him. Scripture reveals man to be completely incompetent to keep the law and commandments of Holy God. "As it is written, "There is none righteous, no, not one ... Therefore by the deeds of the law there shall no flesh be justified in his sight; for by the law is the knowledge of sin" (Romans 3:10, 20). The sin offering was to be an open confession of one's consciousness of sin and unworthiness. "I acknowledge my sin unto thee, and mine iniquity have I not hid ... " (Psalm 32:5a). This acknowledgement places the offerer subject to the unfathomable mercy of God.

The offerer understood this offering to be temporary and a foreshadow of the permanent provision of God for sin. This sin offering was inadequate within itself to forever atone for sin. As Scripture reveals, "For the law having a shadow of good things to come, and not the very image of the things, can never with those sacrifices which they offered year by year continually make the comers thereunto perfect. For then would they have not ceased to be offered? ... But in those sacrifices there is a remembrance again made of sins every year. For it is not possible that the blood of bulls and of goats should take away sins" (Hebrews 10:1-2a, 3-4).

It should be observed that there are four different offerings and four different offerers specified. Because God is fair in His dealings with men, different classes of people and positions of responsibility warranted different sin offerings. The greater the position of the offerer, the greater the sacrifice demanded.

Interestingly, the Holy Spirit mentioned first the priests, Leviticus 4:3. They were definitely not above sin. They were required to offer the most valuable of all animals, the bullock, to atone for their sin. It was not that the sin of the priests was greater, but that they held a greater position of responsibility. This truth is emphasized in James

3:1, "My brethren, be not many masters, knowing that we shall receive the greater condemnation." God places the leadership position of the religious leaders above the civil leaders. The spiritual condition of the religious leaders influenced the spiritual condition of the people, which influenced the spiritual condition of the nation. So much for the separation of church and state!

The next group listed is the 'whole congregation', or the nation, Leviticus 4:13. A bullock was also required as a sacrifice for the sin offering of the populace of Israel. While an individual is responsible for himself, (as described later), if an individual unites with any entity, that individual is placed under a corporate responsibility also. This truth is repeatedly demonstrated throughout the Bible and history. God has judged nations and local church congregations. At times, there may have been individuals who have not participated in the sin of the nation or church, but fall under God's judgment as well. God's judgment fell in A.D. 70 on Jerusalem when it was destroyed by the Romans and the entire nation entered into captivity. "Righteousness exalteth a nation: but sin is a reproach to any people" (Proverbs 14:34). The Lord pronounced pending judgment upon most of the churches listed in Chapters two and three of Revelation. When churches stray from the truth of God's Word, God's judgment will surely come!

When a ruler or civil leader acknowledged his sin he was required to offer a male goat, Leviticus 4:22. This animal was of less worth than the bullock offered by the priests and the congregation, but more valuable than the offering required of an individual. The sin of the ruler was no less than the sin of the priests and congregation, but the ruler was still guilty before Holy God. The ruler's responsibility was not considered as great as the priests' responsibility, but great nonetheless. "Let every soul be subject unto the higher powers. For there is no power but of God: the powers that be are ordained of God … For he is a minister of God to thee for good … " (Romans 13:1, 4a).

The individual would acknowledge his sin by offering a female goat or lamb, Leviticus 4:27, 32. In cases of poverty, the individual was instructed to bring two doves or two pigeons for his sin offering, Leviticus 5:7-10. If the individual was in extreme poverty, he was instructed to present an offering of fine flour, Leviticus 5:11-13. It has been suggested that an offering of fine flour could be used as a sin offering when the priest would burn that which was offered on the altar upon which there was blood, thus giving it the character of a sin offering.[36] From the most affluent to the extremely poor, God made provision for everyone to approach Him and receive atonement of their sin. This sin offering, as in the offerings of the priests, congregation, and the ruler was for a sin of ignorance, which was a sin of omission and definitely a sin against specific commandments of God.

In all the offerings, the sacrifice would lift the guilt complex from the offender and satisfy his conscience. However, this could only be accomplished through the offering of the animal in faith and the shedding of its innocent blood. In each case, the blood would be sprinkled seven times upon the altar; the remainder of the blood poured out at the bottom of the altar; then, the entire body of the animal taken outside the camp and burned at the place of the burnt offering. The Lord acknowledged this would make atonement for them and their sin would be forgiven, Leviticus 4:20b, 26b, 31b, and 35b.

God emphasized the sinfulness of sin in Leviticus 4:11 when He itemized the various parts of the bullock to be offered and burned. The *skin* of the animal would represent the attractiveness of sin. Hebrews 11:25 refers to the "pleasures of sin for a season". The *flesh* would be descriptive of the licentiousness of sin as described in Galatians 5:19-21a. "Now the works of the flesh are manifest, which are these; Adultery, fornication, uncleanness, lasciviousness, idolatry, witchcraft, hatred, variance, emulations, wrath, strife, seditions, heresies, envyings, murders, drunkenness, revellings, and such like ... " The *head* of the animal would emphasize the deliberateness of sin. This was revealed in Genesis 6:5 when God saw in man, " ... that every imagination of the thoughts of his heart was only evil continually." The *legs* of the animal would refer to the waywardness of sin. Scripture states that, "All we like sheep have gone astray; we have turned every one to his own

---

[36] William MacDonald, *Believer's Bible Commentary* (Nashville, Tennessee: Thomas Nelson Publishers, 1985, 1995), 142.

way ... " (Isaiah 53:6). The *inwards* of the animal would reveal to our own innate wickedness, "The heart is deceitful above all things, and desperately wicked: . . ." (Jeremiah 17:9). And finally, the *dung* would be synonymous of the destructiveness and wastefulness of sin. "Then when lust hath conceived, it bringeth forth sin; and sin, when it is finished, bringeth forth death" (James 1:15).[37]

All the sin offering sacrifices pointed to the death of the Messiah. For it is in Christ, "we have redemption through his blood, the forgiveness of sins, according to the riches of his grace" (Ephesians 1:7). It is through death and the shed blood of Christ that one is restored into fellowship and receives the privilege of worship. In Hebrews 9:22a one reads, " ... without the shedding of blood is no remission." Also in 1 John 1:9, God gives this promise, "If we confess our sins, he is faithful and just to forgive our sins, and to cleanse us from all unrighteousness." The sin offering was noted as being 'most holy', Leviticus 6:25, 29. This offering definitely was the most significant of all. Sin must be atoned for before one can approach Holy God.

Although the sin offering and the burnt offering were conducted in the same place, there were some vital contrasts worthy to be reviewed. Dr. J. Vernon McGee submits the following observations worthy to be considered:

> Where the burnt offering leaves off, the sin offering begins. The burnt offering tells *who* Christ is; the sin offering tells what Christ *did*. In the burnt offering Christ meets the demands of God's high and holy standard; in the sin offering Christ meets the deep and desperate needs of man. In the burnt offering we see the preciousness of Christ; in the sin offering we see the hatefulness of sin. The burnt offering was a voluntary offering; the sin offering was commanded. The burnt

---

[37] Stephen F. Olford, *The Tabernacle: Camping With God* (Grand Rapids, Michigan: Kregel Publications, 1971, 2004), 145-146.

offering ascended; the sin offering was poured out. The
one went up and the other went down.[38]

The two compulsory offerings commanded by God to atone for
sin focused on the *nature* of sin, as with the sin offering, and the *act*
of sin, as described in the trespass offering, Leviticus 5:14-6:7; 7:1-
10. The trespass offering required a ram without blemish, with the
addition of restitution to be made by the offender to the offended. God
commanded restitution be made and another one-fifth of the value of
the restitution be added to the repayment. This promoted restoration
of fellowship among the people and encouraged consecration of the
individuals to God. Although there are several specific sins listed in the
above Scripture reference, they are simply a sample and by no means
an exhaustive list.

Through the trespass offering, the Lord teaches that God desires and
delights in obedience to Him and His word. "Behold, to obey is better
than sacrifice, and to hearken than the fat of rams" (1 Samuel 15:22b).
Another truth taught is that God desires unity among believers, Psalm
133:1. Jesus taught in Matthew 5:23-24, "Therefore if thou bring thy
gift to the altar, and there rememberest that thy brother hath ought
against thee; leave there thy gift before the altar, and go thy way; first
be reconciled to thy brother, and then come and offer thy gift." There
is a New Testament example of this practiced in the life and conversion
of Zaccheus in Luke 19:1-10. The true repentance within the heart of
Zaccheus was evidenced in his immediate voluntary restitution to those
he had wronged with an additional fourfold payment. The trespass
offering foreshadows Christ being the center and foundation of man's
reconciliation to God and man, 2 Corinthians 5:17-21.

The Day of Atonement was the most important and significant
day in the nation of Israel, Leviticus 16:1-34; 23:26-32. On this day,
known today as Yom Kippur, atonement for all the sins of the entire
nation would be made. While all the sacrifices and offerings could be
presented each day year round, the Day of Atonement would only be

---

[38] J. Vernon McGee, *Thru The Bible, Vol. 1*, 338

observed once a year. The Lord specified this most important day in the life of Israel to be observed on the tenth day of the seventh month (Tishri, equivalent to September). This was to be a Sabbath of rest and a time of fasting which was required from the evening of the ninth day to the evening of the tenth day.

On the Day of Atonement, only the high priest could enter the tabernacle. All the common priests were forbidden to enter. The high priest would do all the work himself in offering the sacrifice. It was only on this day that the high priest could enter the Holy of Holies. The high priest would wash himself with water and change into the simple attire of white garments. This would symbolize him as unadorned, but pure. Symbolically, Christ put aside His robes of glory and veiled Himself with the flesh of man. He was Man, yet without sin; unadorned, but pure.

The high priest would sacrifice for himself a young bullock for a sin offering and a ram for a burnt offering. This clearly speaks of the holiness of God and the sinfulness of man. At this juncture, there is no correlation between the sacrifice of the high priest for his sin and the work of Christ. Christ is not only the Great High Priest; He is also the sacrifice! Following the sacrifices for himself, the high priest would take two goats, but sacrifice only one goat which was for a sin offering for the nation of Israel.

The high priest would take a basin containing the blood of the sin offering and fill a censer with burning coals from the altar of the burnt offering and place a handful of frankincense upon the hot coals. The smoldering frankincense would release a fragrant smoke that would fill the air, which represented prayer. With the blood and in prayer, he would pass through the veil and enter into the Holy of Holies. When the high priest approached the mercy seat, which was atop the Ark of the Covenant, he would dip his finger into the blood and sprinkle it seven times before the mercy seat. Seven times signified a complete and adequate atonement. One can only imagine the reverent attitude and the awesomeness of this event as the high priest entered into the very presence of God. The high priest would perform his duties meticulously, for he was in the presence of God. Any deviation from these prescribed duties meant instant death. This is a beautiful symbolic picture of Christ entering into the heavenly Holy of Holies. The action of the high priest foreshadows Christ alone as the believer's High Priest and Redeemer.

On the Day of Atonement, an additional element was introduced to the ritual and symbolic foreshadowing of redemption. The second goat would be taken and chosen as a scapegoat. The high priest would lay his hands upon the head of the scapegoat and confess all the sins of the nation of Israel. The scapegoat would be presented alive before the Lord and released into the wilderness, never to be seen again. This beautifully represents the work of the 'Lamb of God' wholly, completely, and entirely removing the sin of the believer. "As far as the east is from the west, so far hath he removed our transgressions from us" (Psalm 103:12). The prophet Isaiah presents God as casting all sin of the believer behind His back, Isaiah 38:17. Micah shares that God symbolically casts all sin of the believer into the depths of the sea, Micah 7:19. The Book of Hebrews states that God does not remember the sin and iniquity of the believer, Hebrews 10:17.

Returning from the Holy of Holies, the high priest would once again wash himself with water and change into his ornate priestly garments. He would send the bodies of the animal sacrifices out of the tabernacle to be completely burned at the place of the burnt offering. The high priest would conclude his work on the Day of Atonement by burning the evening offering of incense and trimming the lamp wicks on the Golden Lampstand. However, each year this same ritual would need to be repeated. Thankfully, the one-time offering of the 'Lamb of God' was sufficient to forever pay for sin.

God had prescribed these offerings and instructions for Israel to follow and to foreshadow to the nations of the world the redemption He was going to provide for humanity. Everything, every animal, and every action had a significant connotation. Especially, the animals to be sacrificed were an important foreshadow of the 'Lamb of God'. God repeatedly emphasized the importance of each animal being without blemish and defect. The responsibility of no defective animal being sacrificed fell upon the priests. In Leviticus 22:17-33, the Lord gave explicit instructions concerning an acceptable sacrifice. Each animal was meticulously examined to ensure the animal met the qualifications specified by the Lord. These animals were be isolated for seven days and scrutinized. If the slightest defect was discovered, the animal was rejected.

Observe the correlations between the foreshadow of these offerings and instructions in Leviticus and the fulfillment of the sacrifice of the 'Lamb of God':

1) The burnt offering pictured complete devotion and surrender to the LORD. It was completely consumed and offered to the LORD as a 'sweet smellingsavour' It was Christ who, "hath given himself for us an offering and a sacrifice to God for a sweetsmelling savor" (Ephesians 5:2). "God is satisfied with Jesus and He sees us in Christ. He is satisfied, then, with us."[39]

2) The grain offering was an offering of thanksgiving to God for His goodness and provision. This pictures the humanity of Christ in all its purity and loveliness. He voluntarily came from heaven and veiled Himself in humanity to present Himself a perfect offering for us. He is the 'Bread of Life' who came from heaven, John 6:48-58.

3) The peace offering was a voluntary offering and a picture of communion and fellowship between individual believers and between believers and God. This aptly pictures the Person of Christ, "For He is our peace, who hath made both one, and hath broken down the middle wall of partition between us" (Ephesians 2:14).

4) The sin offering was the most important offering of all and compulsory. This was the first offering to set forth the work of redemption of Christ. It emphasized the natural sinfulness of man, God's hatred of sin, and man's desperate need of a Savior. The sin offering pictured Christ as man's substitute."For he hath

---

[39] J. Vernon McGee, *Thru The Bible, Vol. 1,* 329.

made him to be sin for us, who knew no sin; that we might be made the righteousness of God in him" (2 Corinthians 5:21).

5) The trespass offering addresses the act of specific sins and is also a compulsory offering. It consisted of confession of the sin, making restitution, if possible, to any offended, and then offer the specified sacrifice. Restitution symbolizes the fruit of repentance. This pictures God's provision through Christ of power and victory over the principle and practice of sin. This could be what Christ was teaching in Matthew 5:23-24 and Luke 19:1-10.

6) The Day of Atonement presents the Lord Jesus Christ as our Great High Priest entering into the Holy of Holies for us, once and for all. "But Christ being come an high priest of good things to come, by a greater and more perfect tabernacle, not made with hands, that is to say, not of this building; neither by the blood of goats and calves, but by his own blood he entered in once into the holy place, having obtained eternal redemption for us" (Hebrews 9:11-12).

7) Each animal presented for sacrifice must pass the meticulous inspection by the priests. Any animal with any flaw or defect would be rejected. This foreshadowed the religious and civil leaders who closely scrutinized Christ throughout His public ministry and the intense examination during His mock trial. Yet, Christ was found without sin and without fault, Hebrews 4:15; John 18:38.

The usual procedure of presenting the various offerings were: first, sin had to be dealt with through the sin or trespass offering; second, one would consecrate or commit himself completely to the LORD through the burnt and grain offerings; third, fellowship would be restored between the Lord, the priest, and the worshipper through the presentation of the peace offering. On the annual Day of Atonement, the scapegoat was included to denote the taking away of the sins of the nation. Remember, atonement means 'to cover'. The sins of the Old Testament believers were expiated, but not taken away until, " ... the Lamb of God which taketh away the sin of the world" (John 1:29). "For the law having a shadow of good things to come, and not the very image of the things, can never with those sacrifices which they offered year by year continually make the comers thereunto perfect ... For it is not possible that the blood of bulls and goats should take away sins" (Hebrews 10:1, 4). The entirety of the offerings and the Day of Atonement presented a comprehensive picture of the foreshadow of the Person and the work of redemption to be accomplished by the coming 'Lamb of God'.

Continue this journey of the foreshadows of the 'Lamb' and observe these truths: "Christ became sin for us on the cross and yet was holy. God withdrew from Him and yet God was in Christ reconciling the world to Himself."[40]

---

[40] J. Vernon McGee, *Thru The Bible, Vol. 1*, 343.

CHAPTER FIVE

Isaiah's Lamb

The search for the next foreshadow of the 'Lamb' recorded within Scripture, takes a quantum leap forward to the prophetic writings of the prophet Isaiah. Isaiah, the prophet, is regarded as chief among the prophets. He compiled his writings over seven hundred years after Moses wrote the Book of Leviticus and approximately seven hundred years prior to the birth of Jesus Christ. Isaiah's preaching and writings present the most undaunted and unparalleled portrait of the vicarious, substitutionary, and atoning foreshadow of the 'Lamb of God' contained within the Old Testament.

The Book of Isaiah has been noted by some scholars as the fifth gospel! It was the writings of Isaiah that the New Testament writers quoted most, with the possible exception to the Psalms. The inauguration of the public ministry of the Lord Jesus Christ began with a reading of prophetic Scripture from the sixty-first chapter of Isaiah. "The Spirit of the Lord is upon me, because he hath anointed me to preach the gospel to the poor; he hath sent me to heal the brokenhearted, to preach deliverance to the captives, and recovering of sight to the blind, to set at liberty them that are bruised, to preach the acceptable year of the Lord" (Luke 4:18-19) (cf. Isaiah 61:1-2a).

Interestingly, the Book of Isaiah contains a striking resemblance of the entire cannon of Scripture, the Bible. The Bible is compiled of sixty-six books; the Book of Isaiah contains sixty-six chapters. The Bible is divided into two sections: the Old Testament and the New Testament; the Book of Isaiah is by some Biblical scholars divided into two sections: chapters one through thirty-nine and chapters forty through sixty-six. The Old Testament deals primarily with judgment and captivity; the first division of Isaiah deals with judgment and captivity. The New Testament deals primarily with grace and salvation; the second division of Isaiah deals with grace and salvation. The Old Testament contains thirty-nine books; the first division of Isaiah contains thirty-nine chapters. The New Testament contains twenty-seven books; the second division of Isaiah contains twenty-seven chapters. The second division of the Book of Isaiah begins as the New Testament does, with the ministry of John the Baptist and ends as the New Testament does, with the new heaven and new earth.

Before delving into the foreshadow of the lamb found in the Book of Isaiah, one should backtrack down the synopsis road and learn of the events that transpired in the life of the nation of Israel from the time of the writing of Book of Leviticus to the writing of the Book of Isaiah. This over-view will enable one to comprehend the context of Isaiah and draw out applicable truths for today.

Forty years after Moses led Israel out of the captivity of Egypt, Joshua led the nation of Israel into the land of Canaan. The Israelites began to conquer the wicked inhabitants of the land, dividing the land among the twelve tribes of Israel, and began to disperse throughout the region. Throughout the days of Joshua, the Hebrew people obeyed and followed Jehovah God. "And the people served the LORD all the days of Joshua, and all the days of the elders that outlived Joshua, who had seen all the great works of the LORD, that he did for Israel … And also that generation were gathered unto their fathers: and there arose another generation after them, which knew not the LORD, nor yet the works which he had done for Israel. And the children of Israel did evil in the sight of the LORD, and served Baalim: And they forsook the LORD God of their fathers, … " (Judges 2:7, 10-12a).

During the next approximately three hundred years Israel experienced a roller coaster ride in their relationship with Jehovah God. The people, as a nation, would forsake their worship of God, fall into apostasy and idolatry, and disobey the clear commands and precepts of God that they had been given. During that time, God used various nations to wage war against Israel and to bring His people to realize they needed Him. God would raise up within Israel judges (military and civil leaders) to call the people to repentance and to call them back to serve Him. These judges would deliver Israel from their enemies, or captors. Each successive judge would continue to lead Israel until his death. Then, the cycle would begin again!

Eventually, the people of Israel demanded of Samuel (the last judge of Israel who was also regarded as a prophet), " ... now make us a king to judge us like all the nations ... And the Lord said unto Samuel, Hearken unto the voice of the people in all they say unto thee: for they have not rejected thee, but they have rejected me, that I should not reign over them" (1 Samuel 8:5b, 7). Samuel obeyed God and the next three leaders of Israel were Kings Saul, David, and Solomon. Unfortunately, at the death of King Solomon, civil war erupted within the nation of Israel. This resulted in the nation being divided into two kingdoms: the northern kingdom which consisted of ten of the twelve tribes of Israel which retained the name Israel; and the southern kingdom which consisted of the last two tribes and became known as Judah.

The northern kingdom, Israel, served twenty different kings, all of which were corrupt and evil. Throughout the reigns of these kings, God would send His prophets to call His people to repentance and for them to return to God and obey and follow Him. Unfortunately, the northern kingdom refused to heed God's gracious and merciful call. This resulted in God lifting His hand of protection from them and allowing the nation of Assyria to engage and defeat them in battle and take Israel into captivity. "For the children of Israel walked in all the sins of Jeroboam which he did; they departed not from them; Until the LORD removed Israel out of his sight, as he had said by all his servants the prophets. So was Israel carried away out of their own land to Assyria unto this day" (2 Kings 17:22-23).

The southern kingdom, Judah, served twenty different kings, but was blessed with several godly kings. These godly kings would bring reform within Judah and re-establish the worship of Jehovah God. God would send various prophets to the nation of Judah, one of whom was Isaiah. Isaiah's message to Judah was a prophetic warning of judgment, but also included the prophetic message of deliverance and salvation. The first chapter of Isaiah provides a summary of enlightenment to the digressed spiritual condition of the southern kingdom of Judah. Chapters two through thirty-nine of Isaiah provide deeper insight to the corruptness of the nation. "Isaiah warned Israel that her wickedness would be punished, and yet God in His grace would one day provide a Savior for both the Jews and the Gentiles."[41]

During the reign of the godly king, Hezekiah, God had graciously and miraculously delivered Judah from the assault of Assyria. However, there was another nation, Babylon, looming in the distance, threatening and striving for world domination. The pending judgment and captivity of Judah prophesied in the first division of Isaiah's writings was the backdrop of the prophesied deliverance and salvation through the Messiah, which is graphically described by Isaiah in chapters 52:13-53:12.

The Old Testament contains the history and progression of mankind in general.

However, the Old Testament's primary focus was on the advancement of the Jewish nation and people of Israel. Jehovah God had covenanted with Abraham to make of him a great nation through which all the nations of the earth would be blessed, Genesis 12:1-3. Through Israel, God desired to show all nations of the world His love and grace. He would give to mankind His written, inspired, and infallible word— the Bible. Through the Jewish people and the lineage of Abraham and King David, God would send the Messiah. Preserved within the Bible, the LORD provided details of the journey of Israel and His interactions with them for our admonition and benefit today. "Now all these things happened unto them for ensamples: and they are written for our admonition, upon whom the ends of the world are come" (1 Corinthians 10:11).

---

[41] William MacDonald, *Believer's Bible Commentary* (Nashville, Tennessee: Thomas Nelson Publishers, 1985, 1995), 938.

The Hebrew people and the nation of Israel had been nourished by God from the time of their conception. Throughout the years, Jehovah God had made them to be a great nation; to be a powerful and important people. Unfortunately, at the time of Isaiah, the prophet, the Hebrew nation had rebelled against God, Isaiah 1:2. Although Isaiah proclaimed prophecies concerning other nations other than Israel and Judah, his primary ministry concentrated on Judah and the entire Hebrew people.

Chapter one of Isaiah provides a summation of God's indictment against Judah and His call to repentance and reconciliation of His people. Through Isaiah, God brings specific and detailed charges of spiritual apostasy against His chosen people. Similar to Moses, Deuteronomy 31:1, Isaiah calls heaven and earth to bear witness against the Israelites and their complacent attitudes of ingratitude and rebellion toward the LORD, Isaiah 1:2. Isaiah spoke of dumb animals, ox and donkey, as having exemplified more gratitude and thankfulness to their owners, than Israel did toward the God who had brought Israel out of the captivity of Egypt, Isaiah 1:3. God's prophet continues to present a bleak and heart wrenching portrait of Israel's spiritual condition at the present time.

Isaiah describes the corporate spiritual apostasy of the nation, Isaiah 1:4-5, utilizing many descriptive terms. Israel had been called to be a 'holy' nation, Exodus 19:6; Isaiah addressed them as a 'sinful' nation; meaning they had missed the mark for the purpose for which God had designed them. God had chosen the Hebrew people to be " ... peculiar people unto himself ... " (Deuteronomy 14:2b); Isaiah described the people as "a people laden with iniquity". The Hebrew word for iniquity, *avon*, carries the meaning of perversity, or morally evil. The Jews were of the 'seed of Abraham', Genesis 17:8; but they had become 'a seed of evildoers'—a people that was harmful, or injurious. God had declared them " ... the children of the LORD your God: ... " (Deuteronomy 14:1a); this generation of Israelites had digressed to become "children that are corrupters" who had allowed their relationship with Holy God to putrefy—to decay with a foul odor. God's specific indictment against Israel was that they had revolted and turned their backs on

God. Scripture described the nation's complete contamination as " ... the whole head is sick, and the whole heart is faint." They had forsaken and departed from Him to such a degree that had provoked God to anger! Dr. J. Vernon McGee offers the following historical digression of any nation:

> there are three steps in the downfall of any nation. There is religious apostasy, then moral awfulness, and finally political anarchy. Many people don't pay attention to the cycle until the stage of political anarchy is reached, and then they cry out that the government should be changed and a new system adopted. Well, the problem is not in the government. The problem in Jerusalem was not in the palace, but the problem was within the temple. The trouble begins when there is spiritual apostasy.[42]

God's charge against Israel was that they were guilty of "having a form of godliness, but denying the power thereof: ... " (2 Timothy 3:5). God had given the Israelites His designed plan of worship through the acceptable sacrifices in His designed temple. There was an acknowledgement of a remnant of people who remained faithful to the LORD. Throughout every generation, God always maintains a faithful remnant of believers. Thus, because of this remnant, the nation had not yet incurred the wrath of God and suffered complete annihilation, as did Sodom and Gomorrah. However, the Hebrew people, as a whole, had turned their backs on God and His truth and now spiritual apostasy dominated the nation.

The people continued to offer sacrifices to God, but their efforts had become more ritualistic, rather than from the heart. Their worship had become meaningless! The sacrifices had lost their significance to the people. This form of worship was abhorrent to Holy God! God called the people's attention to this: "To what purpose is the multitude

---

[42] J. Vernon McGee, *Thru The Bible, Vol. III* (Nashville, Tennessee: Thomas Nelson Publishers, 1982), 190-191.

of your sacrifices unto me? saith the LORD: I am full of the burnt offerings of rams, and the fat of beasts; and I delight not in the blood of bullocks, or of lambs, or of he goats ... Bring no more vain oblations; incense is an abomination unto me; the new moons and sabbaths, the calling of assemblies, I cannot away with; it is iniquity, even the solemn meeting. Your new moons and your appointed feasts my soul hateth: they are a trouble unto me; I am weary to bear them" (Isaiah 1:11-14). Even obedience to God's commands become wrong when the heart of the believer is not in it; evidenced by having no affect in the believer's conduct. Herein is the summation: "Wherefore the Lord said, forasmuch as this people draw near me with their mouth, and with their lips do they honour me, but have removed their heart far from me, and their fear toward me is taught by the precept of men: ... " (Isaiah 29:13). God desires to be worshipped in spirit and in truth, John 4:24.

The Hebrew people had become an ungodly and unholy nation and were facing the judgment and wrath of Holy God. However, because of the merciful grace of God, He extended an invitation of repentance and salvation to them. "Come now, and let us reason together, saith the LORD: though your sins be as scarlet, they shall be white as snow; though they be red like crimson, they shall be as wool" (Isaiah 1:18). The judgment of God was based upon the charges He brought against Israel. God's offer of salvation and deliverance was based upon the work of redemption through the Deliverer and Savior He would send.

All people, like Israel, face the wrath and judgment of God because of sin. All the offerings, sacrifices, and rituals were for the purpose of pointing one to the grace of God and the supreme sacrifice of the 'Lamb of God' who would pay the debt of sin and provide redemption for man. With God, it is never about the ritual; it is all about the heart! The Psalmist wrote, "For thou desirest not sacrifice; else I would give it: thou delightest not in burnt offering. The sacrifices of God are a broken spirit: a broken and contrite heart, O God, thou wilt not despise" (Psalm 51:16-17). The Bible reveals that "all have sinned, and come short of the glory of God" (Romans 3:23). It is revealed that the wages, or price, of sin is death, Romans 6:23. Sin must be paid for before it can be forgiven. "But God commendeth his love toward us, in that, while we were yet sinners, Christ died for us" (Romans 5:8). God extends the invitation to all to come to Him in repentance and faith in Christ for the forgiveness of sin and reconciliation to Him. It is through, and only through, the sacrificial death and shed blood of the 'Lamb of God' that sin can be forgiven and one can be cleansed from all unrighteousness, 1 John 1:9. Salvation is in a Person—the Person of Jesus Christ!

The first thirty-nine chapters of Isaiah continue to reveal the wickedness of the nations and the pending wrath and judgment of God upon the sin. Throughout these chapters, God also continued to issue the call to repentance and salvation to all who would hear and respond.

Chapter forty and the remaining chapters of the Book of Isaiah begin to disclose the future coming of, and the redemptive work of, the Savior—Messiah. Approximately, seven hundred years before the incarnate birth of the Messiah, Isaiah prophesied His coming to suffer for the sin of mankind. Through the writings of the prophet, God presents a vivid portrait of man's Redeemer and the suffering through which salvation would be provided. This descriptive passage of the suffering Savior, Isaiah 52:13 to Isaiah 53:12, is the foundation of gospel theology. Throughout the New Testament, verses from this passage are quoted in relation to the Christ. When comparing Scripture to Scripture, there remains no doubt that this passage refers to the Messiah—the 'Lamb of God'.

The most unarguable and irrefutable proof that this passage, Isaiah 52:13 to 53:12, prophetically refers to the Messiah is found in Acts 8:30-35. Scripture reveals the evangelist, Philip, was led to a very prominent Ethiopian eunuch who had left a worship service in Jerusalem. Philip found the eunuch riding in his chariot and reading from this very passage, Isaiah 53. "The place of the scripture which he read was this, He was led as a sheep to the slaughter; and like a lamb dumb before his shearer, so opened he not his mouth: In his humiliation his judgment was taken away: and who shall declare his generation? for his life was taken from the earth" (Acts 8:32-33) (cf. Isaiah 53:7-8). The Ethiopian asked Philip of whom the prophet was speaking. Scripture records Philip's answer as, "Then Philip opened his mouth, and began at the same scripture, and preached Jesus" (Acts 8:35). Philip knew beyond doubt, as did the educated religious leaders, that the passage in Isaiah 53 prophetically pointed to the promised Messiah! Isaiah 53:1-12 clearly presents the substitutional work of Messiah for the redemption of man. Thus, the title of this chapter, 'Isaiah's Lamb'. It was the Person of Christ who was "brought as a lamb to the slaughter" (Isaiah 53:7b).

Many scholars agree that the passage of Isaiah 52:13-15 should have been included in the fifty-third chapter. These three verses offer a summation of the fifty-third chapter of Isaiah. Isaiah 52:13 introduced the Messiah as, "my servant", or Jehovah's Servant. The title of "my servant" is found in Isaiah 42:1-3. This passage is quoted in Matthew 12:15-20 in reference to the Lord Jesus Christ—Messiah. It is also recorded that the Lord presented Himself as *a servant* in Philippians 2:7, "But made himself of no reputation, and took upon him the form of a servant, and was made in the likeness of men:". The Messiah came in humble submission to His Father's will to redeem mankind. Why is this important? Because bulls, lambs, and goats were not, are not, sufficient substitutes for the eternal payment of man's sin! It required an innocent 'Man' to vicariously suffer for and redeem a guilty man from his sin!

Jehovah's Servant would come as the God-Man! Among the prophecies which speak of this are Genesis 3:15 and Isaiah 7:14. Both make reference to the virgin birth of the Messiah. God Himself would take upon Himself the flesh of man and dwell among men. "In the beginning was the Word, and the Word was with God, and the Word was God … And the Word was made flesh, and dwelt among us … " (John 1:1, 14). The hypostatic union of divinity and humanity would result in the One who would be the perfect sacrifice and substitute.

Upon completion of His sacrificial and redemptive work, *my servant* would be "exalted, and extolled, and be very high" (Isaiah 52:13). This same terminology is used in Isaiah 6:1. The LORD revealed Himself to Isaiah as One who was " … sitting upon a throne, high and lifted up … " Recorded in the New Testament, Peter declared this of Christ, "Therefore being by the right hand of God exalted … " (Acts 2:33). Also, Philippians 2:9 referred to Christ, "Wherefore God also hath high exalted him, and given him a name which is above every other name:". One finds this again in Hebrews1:3, "when he had by himself purged our sins, sat down at the right hand of the Majesty in high;". Thus, Isaiah 52:13 speaks of the divine Messiah and His preeminence!

Isaiah 52:14 is a summary statement of the vicious and horrific suffering Jehovah's Servant would endure. This prophetic statement of the severity of mistreatment and beating resulted in the Messiah's visage (appearance) becoming almost unrecognizable. One receives added enlightenment of this abuse from Isaiah 50:6, "I gave my back to the smiters, and my cheeks to them that plucked off the hair: I hid not my face from shame and spitting." Although, the fifty-third chapter of Isaiah provides more insight concerning the suffering of our Savior, God graciously veiled in darkness the intense and brutal ugliness of His suffering. Making reference to the Messiah's suffering, "And it was about the sixth hour, and there was a darkness over all the earth until the ninth hour. And the sun was darkened … " (Luke 23:44-45a).

The conclusion of the summary found in Isaiah 52:15 provides enlightenment of the future effect of, and the revelation and reception of, the truth that men had rejected the true Messiah. This Scripture first reveals Messiah's power to purify those who trust in Him and receive His gift of redemption. "Let us draw near with a true heart in full assurance of faith, having our hearts sprinkled from an evil conscience, and our bodies washed with pure water" (Hebrews 10:22). "And to Jesus the mediator of the new covenant, and to the blood of sprinkling, that speaketh better things than that of Abel" (Hebrews 12:24). Peter wrote concerning the sprinkling, " … through sanctification of the Spirit, unto obedience and sprinkling of the blood of Jesus Christ: … " (1 Peter 1:2).

The astonishment of the rejecters of the Messiah is revealed in the latter portion of Isaiah 52:15. There will come a time when all opposition will be silenced and all will acknowledge Christ, the Messiah. "Wherefore God also hath highly exalted him, and given him a name which is above every name: that at the name of Jesus every knee should bow, of things in heaven, and things in earth, and things under the earth; and that every tongue should confess that Jesus Christ is Lord, to the glory of God the Father" (Philippians 2:9-11).

It is in Isaiah 52:13 through Isaiah 53:12 that the sacrificial, substitutionary, and redemptive work of the 'Lamb of God' is prophetically described. Fruchtenbaum presents an interesting observation concerning this passage:

> It is quite common today to hear rabbis say that this passage speaks, not of Messiah, but of Israel suffering in a Gentile world. They may even go so far as to say that this has always been the traditional view of Judaism. At that point they are entirely dependent upon the ignorance of their listeners. All of the ancient Jewish writings – the *Mishnah*, the *Gemara*, (the *Talmud*), the *Midrashim* and many others – all regard this portion of Scripture as relating to the Messianic Person. The first rabbi to suggest otherwise was Rashi, around 1050 A.D. Every rabbi prior to Rashi without exception, viewed this passage as describing Messiah.[43]

Interestingly, Fruchtenbaum observes that the Messiah would initially be rejected by Israel, Isaiah 49, but eventually would be accepted. The passage recorded in Isaiah 53 is the future confession and acceptance of Messiah by Israel. "This description of Messiah, then, is not given as something still to happen, but from a point of time in the future, immediately prior to Messiah's Second Coming, looking back to his First Coming."[44] Therefore, though Isaiah 53 records the most profound and detailed Old Testament prophecy of the vicarious, substitutional, atoning, and sacrificial death of Messiah, the Servant of Jehovah, it is also the future recognition and confession of the nation of Israel of the Messiah whom they had long rejected—Jesus Christ.

The prophet presents the Person of Jehovah's Servant in Isaiah 53:1-3 by asking a rhetorical question: "Who hath believed our report?" Isaiah acknowledges the unbelief and rejection of Israel evidenced toward

---

[43] Arnold G. Fruchtenbaum, *Messianic Christology* (San Antonio, Texas: Ariel Ministries, 1998), 54.

[44] Arnold G. Fruchtenbaum. *Messianic Christology*. 54.

the Messiah. Though the Jews were knowledgeable of the prophetic Messianic Scriptures, they failed to recognize the arrival of Messiah. Throughout Isaiah's writings, he repeatedly referred to the 'arm of the LORD'. The prophet declared the 'arm of the LORD' would rule for God in Isaiah 40:10. Isaiah indicates the Gentiles will trust in the 'arm of the LORD' in Isaiah 51:5. One reads in Isaiah 51:9 that it will be the 'arm of the LORD' that will redeem. In Isaiah 52:10, one learns it will be the 'arm of the LORD' that will provide salvation. The 'arm of the Lord' is revealed in Isaiah 52:13–Isaiah 53:12, to be the same as 'Jehovah's Servant'—Messiah. Yet, Israel refused to receive a Messiah who would suffer and die; for they were looking for a different kind of Messiah. They were looking for a militant King who would deliver them out of their oppression. The New Testament Scriptures found in John 1:11-13 reveal the reception of Israel, and mankind in general, of the Messiah. "He came unto his own, and his own received him not. But as many as received him, to them gave he power to become the sons of God, even to them that believe on his name. Which were born, not of blood, nor of the will of the flesh, nor of the will of man, but of God."

Another reason Israel rejected Jehovah's Servant was the method in which He entered the scene of humanity; He came in an ordinary and normal way. Messiah came as a child born into a poor family; He was born without the obvious prestige of royalty and position. Isaiah prophesied in 53:2, that He would be one who would come as a child and mature as a normal man without the pomp and circumstance that would draw unusual attention to Himself. He would grow as a tender plant (a child), as a root in a dry ground (the nation of Israel). Throughout the life of Messiah, the Heavenly Father would acknowledge on more than one occasion, "This is my beloved Son, in whom I am well pleased" (Matthew 3:17b).

When Israel looked upon Jehovah's Servant, they saw only a simple and humble man. He was man—the God-Man! In His life, He was subjected to the same rejection, scorn, problems, temptations, sorrows, and grief of all humanity, Isaiah 53:3. Yet, He was without sin! However, all people in general, rejected Him and did not bestow upon Him the respect due Him as the Royalty of Heaven. "He was in the world, and the world was made by him, and the world knew him not" (John 1:10).

In Isaiah 53:4-6, the prophet disclosed the passion (suffering) of Jehovah's Servant. Through Isaiah, God very vividly revealed the vicarious substitutionary sacrifice of His Servant for the sin of humanity. Isaiah prophetically looked forward to the crucifixion of Jehovah's Servant and His sufferings. The prophet also prophetically revealed the blindness and the future confession of Israel of the death of man's Messiah. Initially, Israel looked upon the suffering and death of Christ as Him being afflicted, punished, by God for His own sin. However, it was prophesied that Israel, as well as all people, will one day confess that Messiah suffered and died for, not His sin, but their sin. "Surely, he hath borne our griefs, and carried our sorrows: ... " (Isaiah 53:4a).

The substitutionary death of Christ is clearly emphasized in Isaiah 53:5-6. At that time, God would fulfill His statement to Abraham that, " ... God will provide himself a lamb ... " (Genesis 22:8a). Notice how the truth of this substitution is borne out in Isaiah's Scriptures: He has 'borne *our* griefs', 'carried *our* sorrows', He was 'wounded for *our* transgressions', was 'bruised for *our* iniquities', 'the chastisement of *our* peace was upon him', and with 'his stripes *we* are healed'.

Scriptures reveal that all the world is guilty before Holy God in Romans 3:19, and in James 4:4a, " ... the friendship with the world is enmity with God." Though this enmity exists, Paul assures us in Romans 5:1 that peace can be achieved through Christ, "Therefore being justified by faith, we have peace with God through our Lord Jesus Christ." According to Colossians 1:20, it was Jesus Christ who "made peace through the blood of his cross." Peter was inspired to present the truth that it was Jesus Christ, "Who his own self bare our sin in his own body on the tree, that we, being dead to sins, should live unto righteousness: by whose stripes we are healed" (1 Peter 2:24). The healing of man's spiritual condition is also referred to in Isaiah 19:22 and Jeremiah 3:22. Praise God, through the sacrifice of Christ, we are healed of our trespasses and sin!

All of mankind, not just Israel, is reckoned with the same spiritual need. Notice in Isaiah 53:6, this verse begins with the same word in which it ends—*all*. All men, Jews and Gentiles, have the same basic sin problem and God has provided the same remedy, redemption, for all! It was for mankind, not Himself, that Jehovah's Servant, Christ, died. "The LORD hath laid on him the iniquity of us all." As our substitute, the Innocent died for the guilty! This substitution is described in 2 Corinthians 5:21 as, "For he hath made him to sin for us, who knew no sin; that we might be made the righteousness of God in him."

W. E. Vine offers the following observation and summation of Isaiah 53:4-6:

> What the nation will hereafter acknowledge is true of the whole human race. Man has substituted his own will for God's will. Being granted the power of self-determination, a feature which, among others, marks him as made in the image of God, he has used that power to go "his own way" and make himself ego-centric instead of God-centric.
>
> In this universal condition of guilt and misery the grace of God has interposed. Sending his own Son "in the likeness of sinful flesh and as an offering for sin" (Rom. 8:3, R.V.), He made to meet upon Him the whole weight of our iniquity and the righteous wrath due to it.[45]

The manner in which Jehovah's Servant approached His substitutionary suffering is recorded in Isaiah 53:7-9. His humble and submissive passivity is described twice in verse seven as One who "opened not his mouth". As a lamb led to slaughter, Messiah voluntarily gave Himself to be a ransom for many. Throughout the mock trial and the physical abuse He undeservingly endured, Christ Jesus never spoke in His defense concerning the false accusations levied against Him. The Jewish leadership, Herod, and Pilate all marveled at the silence of Jesus Christ: Matthew 26:63, 27:12-14; Mark 14:61, 15:5; and Luke

---

[45] W. E. Vine, *Isaiah: Prophecies, Promise, Warnings* (Grand Rapids, Michigan: Zondervan Publishing House, Paperback Edition, 1971), 168-169.

23:9. Peter described Jesus Christ's silence as One, "Who knew no sin, neither was there guile found in his mouth: Who, when he was reviled, reviled not again; when he suffered, he threatened not; but committed himself to him that judgeth righteously" (1 Peter 2:22-23). He knew the purpose for which He came. Apart from the 'Lamb's' suffering and sacrifice, man would have no hope!

Jehovah's Servant would be meticulously examined and interrogated by both the religious and civil authorities, but would be found without fault. Although Messiah's accusers would be unable to find justifiable charges against Him, they nonetheless condemned Him to die. Scriptures reveal Messiah, " ... hath poured out his soul unto death: and he was numbered with the transgressors" (Isaiah 53:12b). Isaiah stated, " ... for the transgression of my people was he stricken" (Isaiah 53:8c). The phrase 'my people' refers to Israel. Fruchtenbaum offers the following insights:

> Messiah will be killed for the sins of Israel. Here for the first time in Scripture it clearly states that Messiah is to die. There have been many previous references to His suffering, but it was never suggested that He would die. It is important to remember that Messianic prophecy was a progressive revelation.[46]

God thwarted the intentions of the religious rulers to have the body of Messiah ignominiously buried with the two robbers with whom He was crucified. Because Messiah had done no violence and there was no deceit in his mouth, God vindicated Messiah and orchestrated His body buried with the rich. "And ye know that he was manifested to take away our sins; and in him is no sin" (1 John 3:5). A rich man, Joseph of Arimathea, requested of Pilate, the Roman Governor, and received permission to bury the body of Messiah. Joseph buried Jesus Christ's body in the tomb that he had prepared for himself, Matthew 27:57-60.

---

[46] Arnold G. Fruchtenbaum, *Messianic Christology*, 56.

Isaiah made a very startling and definitive statement concerning the suffering and death of His Servant. "Yet it pleased the LORD to bruise him; he hath put him to grief" (Isaiah 53:10). The death of Messiah would not be due to happenstance, to circumstance, for a crime He had committed, or because He was at the wrong place at the wrong time, but because it was the eternal divine plan of Almighty Holy God. Jehovah God was ultimately responsible for the death of Christ! Jesus Christ knew why He came upon the scene of humanity, " ... but for this cause came I unto this hour" (John 12:27). "It was not what Jesus endured at the hands of men that made reconciliation for man's sin, but what He endured at the hand of God!"[47] The first three hours Christ hung upon the cross, He suffered the shame and agony inflicted by men. It was the final three hours, noon to three in the afternoon, that Christ suffered as no man ever has, nor ever will. Jesus "delivered us from the wrath to come" (1 Thessalonians 1:10b).

It was within those final three hours that Jesus Christ, who knew no sin, was made to be sin for man. Messiah suffered the holy and righteous wrath of God for the sin of *all* men: past, present, and future! At this time, the sun was darkened and the full extent of the wrath of God endured by the Son of God was veiled from men. The Holy Son of God became sin! He did not simply bear the sin, He became sin! Here a 'mystery of the gospel' is seen: Christ had never experienced sin; but, by the grace of God, He became sin! Yet, He remained holy! At this time, God withdrew from Christ and yet, God was in Christ reconciling the world to Himself, 2 Corinthians 5:19. This was a mysterious work of God! This unfathomable and incomprehensible suffering would release the agonizing cry of the only begotten Son, "My God, My God, why hast thou forsaken me?" (Mark 15:34) (cf. Psalm 22:1). The price of sin would be paid for by the death and shed blood of the 'Lamb of God'! Holy God, the Father, offered His only Son, the promised Son, as the only acceptable substitute and sacrifice for sinful man. Christ would die as an "offering for sin" (Isaiah 53:10c); "he shall bear their iniquity"

---

[47] H. A. Ironside, *The Prophet Isaiah* (Neptune, New Jersey: Loizeaux Brothers, 1952, Eleventh Printing 1975), 304.

(Isaiah 53:11b); and He would "bare the sin of many" (Isaiah 53:12d). It would be upon the cross that the 'Lamb of God' would take away the sin of the world!

God declared the sufficiency of the sacrifice of His Servant. "He shall see the travail of his soul, and shall be satisfied:" (Isaiah 53:11a). Upon the cross, Christ cried out "it is finished" (John 19:30), referring to all that was needed to be done for redemption of man had been done! It was of the sacrificial shed blood of Christ to which Scripture refers, "But this man, after he had offered one sacrifice for sins for ever, sat down at the right hand of God" (Hebrews 10:12). Salvation would be offered to, "him that worketh not, but believeth on him that justifieth the ungodly, his faith is counted for righteousness" (Romans 4:5).

As Isaiah prophesies of the sacrificial death of Jehovah's Servant, he quickly prophesies of His resurrection. The following phrases indicate this truth: "he shall see his seed"; "he shall prolong his days"; "my righteous servant shall justify many". The resurrection of Jesus Christ on the third day as He predicted, Matthew 16:21, validated everything Jesus had done and said. Christ's empty tomb testified of Jesus' deity and the satisfaction of Jehovah with His redemptive work. Jesus Christ was "declared to be the Son of God with power, according to the spirit of holiness, by the resurrection from the dead" (Romans 1:4).

In conclusion, the prophet makes reference to the ascension of Jehovah's Servant. He would make "intercession for the transgressors" (Isaiah 53:12d). Jehovah's Servant would be exalted, extolled, and be very high, Isaiah 52:13! Because Christ ascended to the right hand of Jehovah God, "He is able also to save them to the uttermost that come to God by him, seeing he ever liveth to make intercession for them" (Hebrews 7:25).

Note the following correlations between 'Isaiah's Lamb' and the 'Lamb of God':

1) 'Isaiah's Lamb' came as a child and matured as a normal man without the obvious prestige of royalty and position that would

draw unusual attention to Himself, Isaiah 53:2; as did the Messiah, Luke 2:40, 52.

2) 'Isaiah's Lamb' became supreme substitute and sacrifice for our sin and redemption, Isaiah 53:4-6; as did Jehovah's Servant, 2 Corinthians 5:21; John 1:29.

3) 'Isaiah's Lamb' offered no resistance to His oppressors, defense to His innocence, or retaliation for His affliction; neither did the 'Lamb of God', 1 Peter 2:22-23. He voluntarily offered Himself as an innocent substitute for sinful and guilty man, Isaiah 53:7.

4) 'Isaiah's Lamb', as well as the Messiah, would die and be buried in a rich man's tomb, 1 John 3:5; Matthew 27: 57-60.

5) 'Isaiah's Lamb' and the 'Lamb of God' would purposefully be sacrificed by God, the Father as an 'offering for sin', Isaiah 53:10; Mark 15:34.

6) 'Isaiah's Lamb': His sacrifice would be accepted as a sufficient payment for sin and provide justification to all who trust Him, Isaiah 53:11; as would the sacrifice of Christ Jesus, Ephesians 1:7; Titus 3:5-7.

7) 'Isaiah's Lamb' would be resurrected and become the justifier of all who would come to God by Him, Isaiah 53:11; as would Christ Jesus, Romans 4:5.

8) 'Isaiah's Lamb' would ascend to the right of God to forever make intercession for those who believe, Isaiah 53:12d; as would Christ Jesus, Hebrews 7:25.

Everything about Isaiah 52:13 to Isaiah 53:12 speaks of the vicarious and substutionary work of redemption of the Messiah—Jehovah's Servant, the 'Lamb of God'. Although Israel did not recognize or receive

Messiah when He first came to live among them; they will confess Him, Jesus Christ, as their Messiah upon His second advent. Though there are some Jews who confess Christ as Messiah now, the entire Jewish nation will one day confess Him. Paul wrote, "I would not, brethren, that ye should be ignorant of this mystery, lest ye should be wise in your own conceits, that blindness in part is happened to Israel, until the fulness of the Gentiles be come in. And so all Israel shall be saved: as it is written, There shall come out of Sion the Deliverer, and shall turn away ungodliness from Jacob: For this is my covenant unto them, when I shall take away their sins" (Romans 11:25-27).

The major truth of Isaiah 53 is that all of Jehovah's Servant's sufferings and His death would be substitutionary. He died so those who believe in Him would have eternal life! He died to take away man's sin! He died to provide a way for all to have a new relationship with Holy God! Jesus said, "I am the way, the truth, and the life: no man cometh unto the Father, but by me" (John 14:6). Christ Jesus would be and is the only sufficient and acceptable sacrifice for man's sin.

The journey down the redemptive crimson path will now begin to focus on the *fulfillment* of the foreshadows that have been observed. How did the One who was initially introduced as 'God's Lamb' meet the requirements of becoming the acceptable sacrifice?

Chapter Six

God's Lamb

Have you noticed that in this journey through the foreshadows the path has been blood stained? Each foreshadow necessitated the requirement of the shedding of innocent and pure blood for the sin of the guilty. The crimson flow beginning in the Garden, flows throughout the Old Testament, connecting each of the foreshadows of the Lamb. Entering into the New Testament, the 'mystery of the Gospel' begins to unfold and God's plan of redemption comes to fruition. The crimson river runs deep with the blood of the 'Lamb of God'!

Fast forward to the New Testament and begin to examine the fulfillment of the foreshadows presented in the previous chapters. Pause and recap some of the truths discovered in the foreshadows concerning the purpose of the 'Lamb of God'. Scripture reveals that God would provide Himself a Lamb! 'God's Lamb' would provide the proper covering by which to approach Holy God; would be innocent and free from the guilt of sin; would be sinless and perfect; would be a perfect Man to be substituted for guilty man; would vicariously suffer the righteous wrath of Holy God for the payment of sin for all mankind; would die a physical death; would be resurrected from the dead; and would ascend to heaven and be exalted above all!

Herein was a great dilemma! There was no perfect, innocent, or sinless man! God had declared there was none who was good. "The LORD looked down from heaven upon the children of men, to see if there were any that did understand and seek God. They are all gone aside, they are all together become filthy: there is none that doeth good, no, not one" (Psalm 14:2-3). However, before the foundations of the world, God looked down through the eons of time and foresaw the redemptive need of sinful man. Almighty God had a plan to reconcile man unto Himself and redeem man from their sin, 1 Peter 1:17-21. This plan was birthed from God's love and unmerited grace. As prescribed in God's law, the sacrifice had to be the best, without blemish, without flaw, completely innocent, without sin—perfect! Man's redemption depended on the appropriate sacrifice!

This chapter, concerning 'God's Lamb', will focus on God's choice of the One who would meet His requirements and how that was manifested through the life of the Chosen One. The following chapters will examine the Lamb's sacrifice and exaltation.

Therefore, before the foundations of the world and the creation of man, God, the Father (first person of the Trinity) predetermined to send God, the Son (second person of the Trinity) into the world to be man's Redeemer. The Son volunteered to come to suffer death on earth and to rescue mankind from the wrath of Holy God as man's substitute and payment for sin. "Blessed be the God and Father of our Lord Jesus Christ, who hath blessed us with all spiritual blessings in heavenly places: According as he hath chosen us in him before the foundation of the world, that we should be holy and without blame before him in love: Having predestined us unto the adoption of children by Jesus Christ to himself, according to the good pleasure of his will, to the praise of the glory of his grace, wherein he hath made us accepted in the beloved. In whom we have redemption through his blood, the forgiveness of sins, according to the riches of his grace" (Ephesians 1:3-7).

God, the Son, would not come as God; but as a Man. He would be God incarnate; God in human flesh! Deity would unite with humanity. This is referred to as the hypostatic union. Walvoord defines this union:

> Because the attributes of either nature belong to Christ,
> Christ is theanthropic in nature, but it is not accurate to
> refer to His natures as being theanthropic as there is no

mixture of the divine and human to form a new third substance. The human nature always remains human, and the divine nature always remains divine. Christ is therefore both God and Man, no less God because of His humanity and no less human because of His deity.[48]

Man's Redeemer would be one hundred percent God and one hundred percent Man! John described the union as, "In the beginning was the Word, and the Word was with God, and the Word was God. The same was in the beginning with God ... And the Word was made flesh, and dwelt among us, (and we beheld his glory, the glory as of the only begotten of the Father,) full of grace and truth" (John 1:1-2, 14).

All the names by which the Redeemer was referred to in the Old Testament Scriptures are synonymous to the New Testament name, Jesus. The fulfillment of all the foreshadows of the Lamb would be found in none other than the Son of God—Jesus Christ! "For God so loved the world, that he gave his only begotten Son, that whosoever believeth in him should not perish, but have everlasting life. For God sent not his Son into the world to condemn the world; but that the world through him might be saved" (John 3:16-17). God's only begotten Son, Jesus Christ, qualified to be 'God's Lamb', chosen to be the ultimate sacrifice and payment for the sin of mankind!

Though there would be a change of a very limited manifestation of Christ's divine nature throughout His humanity, no attribute of His divine nature would be changed, nor diminished. This self-emptying of Christ is sometimes referred to as the kenosis doctrine. Even though Jesus Christ had chosen to limit certain phases of His divine attributes within His human ministry, He remained all that God is! The importance of Jesus as the God-Man is described by Walvoord, "As Man Christ could die, but only as God could His death have infinite value sufficient to provide redemption for the sins of the whole world. Thus the human

---

[48] John F. Walvoord, *JESUS CHRIST OUR LORD* (Chicago, Illinois: Moody Publishers, 1996), 115.

blood of Christ has eternal and infinite value because it was shed as part of the divine-human Person."[49]

Scriptures record the prophecies of the peculiar entrance of deity into humanity. Among these are Genesis 3:15, when God referred to the "Seed of the woman" and when Isaiah spoke of a virgin giving birth to a Son, Isaiah 7:14. A virgin giving birth! Unheard of, absolutely impossible! However, "with God nothing shall be impossible" (Luke 1:37). Written within the leaf of one of this writer's Bibles is the following quotation of R. L. Moyer: "God made man (Adam) without a woman or a man; God brought forth a motherless woman (Eve) from the body of a man; God brought forth a fatherless man (Jesus) from the body of a woman." God had proven His ability to make phenomenal births occur through the examples of the initial creation of Adam, the birth of Isaac, and as a contemporary to Jesus, the miraculous birth of John the Baptist to the elderly couple, Zacharias and Elizabeth, Luke 1:5-25, 57-63. The incarnation of Christ was essential, for if Jesus Christ had been born of a man and a woman, He would have inherited the same sin nature as everyone else born into this world—eliminating Him as the perfect sacrifice! "But when the fulness of the time was come, God sent forth his Son, made of a woman, made under the law, to redeem them that were under the law, that we might receive the adoption of sons" (Galatians 4:4-5).

What was meant by the phrase, "the fulness of time" (Galatians 4:4)? It was the time in history when the progression of humanity reached an established point; whereby, it was conducive for God to send His Son to earth. It was the time in history when the Romans had obtained dominance. It was when the common vernacular throughout the vast Roman Empire was the Koine Greek language which provided continuity of communication. The Romans made travel easier with the infrastructure of an adequate road system throughout the empire. The legal structure of Rome perfected the lethal capital punishment used for all malefactors throughout the empire, the crucifixion. History records the Romans use of their 'Acta Diurna', their early version of what we now call our newspaper allowing mass communication of events. The

---

[49] John F. Walvoord, *JESUS CHRIST OUR LORD*, 120.

Romans introduced the codex: a process that involved the stacking of various pages of documentation, binding them together; thus, becoming the earliest resemblance of a book. This became the foundation of the preservation of the sacred writings. All things were in place for the Son of God to enter upon the scene of humanity and for His message to be delivered throughout the world.

Serious Jewish students of Scripture were anxiously anticipating the arrival of Messiah. They calculated that according to the prophetic statement in Daniel 9:24-25, four hundred and eighty-three years from the event of the rebuilding of Jerusalem, Messiah would come. This rebuilding was authorized during the reign of Cyrus, the Persian king, 538 B.C., 2 Chronicles 36:23-24. However, the command to rebuild did not occur until 445 B.C., when Artaxerxes issued the commandment in the days of Nehemiah, Nehemiah 2:1-8.

Although, the Jewish nation anxiously anticipated the arrival of Messiah, they looked for and longed for Messiah to come and militarily deliver them from their oppressors. The Jews did not consider themselves in need of a Redeemer from sin, because they were of the 'seed' of Abraham. However, God is always concerned with an individual's spiritual condition more than their pedigree.

In the days of Jesus Christ, the only Scriptures available were what are now known as the Old Testament. The Jewish teachers taught, and readily received, that the expected and anticipated Savior, or Messiah, would come to overthrow the Jew's enemies and establish His kingdom on earth. The early rabbis concluded the Scriptures spoke of two different Messiahs. Fruchtenbaum offers the following insight into the human logic behind this conclusion:

> The Messiah who was to come, suffer and die was termed Messiah, Son of Joseph, *Mashiach ben Yoseph*. The second Messiah, who would then come following the first, was termed Messiah, Son of David, *Mashiach ben David*. This one would raise the first Messiah back to life, and establish the Messianic Kingdom of peace on earth ... For centuries Orthodox Judaism held the

concept of two Messiahs. Since the Talmudic period, however, in the history of the Jewish people, the Son of David alone was played up in the imaginations of Jewish hearts and minds. The other messianic figure, Messiah, the Son of Joseph, the suffering one, was ignored.[50]

The early rabbis failed to understand the truth that the same Messiah would come twice; first to suffer as man's Savior and second to reign victorious as King.

Approximately seven hundred years from the writings of Isaiah, the prophet, the Scriptures introduced a young Jewish man, Joseph, and his fiancé, Mary, Luke 1:26-38. In strict adherence to Jewish custom, Joseph and Mary would observe an engagement period of one year. A Jewish engagement was as binding as a marriage with the same responsibilities and benefits, with the exception of the couple living together before the actual wedding. It was during this engagement period, the angel Gabriel announced to the virgin Mary, that she had been chosen by God to be the one through whom His Son would be born and enter into this world. Although Mary was engaged to Joseph, she questioned how she, a virgin, would give birth. The angel gave this response: "The Holy Ghost shall come upon thee, and the power of the Highest shall overshadow thee: therefore also that holy thing which shall be born of thee shall be called the Son of God" (Luke 1:35). Mary humbly and obediently responded, "Behold, the handmaid of the Lord; be it unto me according to thy word" (Luke 1:38).

Joseph's world was shaken to its foundation when Mary, his beloved, informed him of the news of her pregnancy and the pending birth of Messiah! Should he believe her preposterous story about the angel's visit and being pregnant with child while remaining a virgin? How was he to respond to that? Within the Jewish culture, news of an unwed pregnancy carried tremendous and devastating consequences. If it was determined that Mary had committed adultery, Joseph could divorce

---

[50] Arnold G. Fruchtenbaum, *Messianic Christology* (San Antonio, Texas: Ariel Ministries, 1998), 123.

her and she could be legally stoned to death. If it was determined that Joseph and Mary had committed fornication (sex before marriage), they would incur the stigma of an illegitimate birth of their child. Their reputations, which were held in high esteem, would be marred.

Joseph quietly and deliberately contemplated his options. What should he do? Should he divorce Mary, breaking their engagement? If he did, he did not desire any harm to come to her. Finally, he concluded he would privately end their engagement to avoid bringing any undue attention to the situation. As he deliberated on his future actions, the angel, Gabriel, appeared to him in a dream, Matthew 1:18-25. In response to Gabriel's assurance that the message Mary had conveyed to him was true, Joseph placed the will and plan of God ahead of his own. He would follow through with the marriage and would willingly raise the child that he had not fathered.

Obedience to the will of God is rewarding; but, many times results in great sacrifice and is sometimes painful! Joseph and Mary were looking at the unknown. Without doubt, many questions must have flooded their minds; but, they loved each other and they loved their God! They looked at their future through the eyes of faith. Their journey would possibly be difficult, but they would trust their God! All the misunderstandings, injustices, shame, and humiliation this young couple were to endure would become "a foreshadowing of the injustice that the innocent Son of God would endure on our behalf."[51]

Jesus could have entered humanity in glorious splendor with all the accolades due the God of creation, or any other way He chose. However, God chose to send Christ through the innocence of a new born babe. Thus, fulfilling the foreshadow of the innocence of the Lamb chosen for our substitutionary sacrifice.

Jesus' birth came without much fanfare. The Promised Messiah, God's Son, was born in a cave used to shelter the cattle. Mary lovingly placed her precious babe in the only available crib; a hewn out rock used as the cattle's feeding trough. Ironically, this baby, the royalty of heaven,

---

[51] Charles R. Swindoll, *The Greatest Life of All: Jesus* (Nashville, Tennessee: Thomas Nelson, Inc., 2008), 29.

would have no fitting place to lay His head His entire earthy life, Matthew 8:20. No one on earth except Joseph and Mary, unless perhaps animals seeking shelter for the night, witnessed the birth of the Messiah into the world. However, all of Heaven was rocking with jubilation as angelic voices proclaimed Christ's arrival, not to the elite crowd or kings, but to lowly shepherds as they watched over their flocks that glorious night, Luke 2:8-20. In response to the angel's announcement, the shepherds found the new born babe and told Joseph and Mary and all who would listen of the angel's message concerning this child—God had sent a Savior!

Sometime after the birth of Jesus, a few wise men from the east, magi, came to pay tribute to the newly arrived 'King of the Jews', Matthew 2:12. The magi found the young child, not a babe, and Mary in a house, not His birthplace. The magi worshipped Jesus and presented the Child with gifts of gold, frankincense, and myrrh. "The early church fathers understood the gold to be symbolic of Christ's deity, the frankincense of His purity, and the myrrh of His death (since it was used for embalming)."[52] Had the magi presented their gifts immediately after the birth of Jesus, as tradition implies, Joseph and Mary could have used the gold to purchase a lamb for their offering when they presented the eight day old baby, Jesus, unto the Lord, Luke 2:21-24. Instead, they offered the fowls which were allowed by Levitical law for those of poverty. This affirms that the Christ child was born into a family of poor and humble standing.

When Joseph and Mary presented baby Jesus unto the Lord in the temple, they were approached by a devout man, Simeon, and an elderly prophetess, Anna. Simeon had received revelation from God that he would be permitted to see the promised Messiah before he died. Upon seeing Jesus, Simeon took the babe in his arms and praising God, he acknowledged His faithfulness: "Lord, now lettest thou thy servant depart in peace, according to thy word: For mine eyes have seen thy salvation, which thou hast prepared before the face of all people; a light to lighten the Gentiles, and the glory of thy people Israel" (Luke

---

[52] Charles Ryrie, *Ryrie Study Bible, King James Version,* 1419. Notes on Matthew 2:11.

2:29-32). Simeon continued speaking to Mary and foretold of the joy and anguish that she would experience through the life and death of her Son. Anna had served the Lord in the temple through prayer and fastings while looking for the Redeemer. Upon seeing baby Jesus, she immediately gave thanks and began testifying to all that Jesus was the promised Redeemer, Luke 2:36-38. Unfortunately, most of Israel was so spiritually blinded by the traditional teachings of their religious leaders that they did not heed the testimonies of the shepherds, Simeon, and Anna. Israel was looking for a militant Messiah, not a baby! Most failed to realize their need for a spiritual Redeemer.

The early years of Jesus' life have been shrouded in mystery, for the Scriptures provide only a glimpse into the boyhood years of Jesus. The only insight into the early years of Jesus are found in Luke 2:39-52. Within this passage, the Scriptures reveal that Jesus developed and grew the same as any other child, "And the child grew, and waxed strong in spirit, filled with wisdom: and the grace of God was upon him ... And Jesus increased in wisdom and stature, and in favor with God and man" (Luke 2:40, 52). This passage also unveils an incident involving an encounter between the young Jesus and the scholarly religious leaders in the temple in Jerusalem. Although He was only twelve years old, Jesus amazed these learned teachers of Israel with His questions and the answers He gave to their questions. "And all that heard him were astonished at his understanding and answers" (Luke 2:47). Jesus acknowledged to Mary that He was already about the business of His Father. "It is striking that these first recorded words of Jesus are of a piece with his entire life and mission: he must be about God's business."[53] At the tender age of twelve, if not earlier, Jesus already knew and understood the divine purpose for which He came.

The narrative of the life of Jesus jumps from His encounter in the temple to His baptism, eighteen years later. When Jesus was thirty years of age, He presented Himself to the prophet, John the Baptist, to be baptized, Matthew 3:13-17. Although John the Baptist was a preacher of

---

[53] Paul Johnson, *Jesus: A Biography from a Believer* (New York, New York: The Penguin Group, 2010), 27.

repentance which was expressed through the rite of baptism, Jesus had something else in mind and changed the symbolism of baptism forever. Swindoll offers the following observations:

> The rite of baptism also had another meaning that would be important to Jesus. It was the rite of priests who were purified by the washing of water just prior to representing the people before God in the Most Holy Place … That day, Jesus officially began a journey that would lead to His ultimate destiny. His ritual cleansing publicly announced the beginning of His ministry— the pursuit of His call. And His first act was to make baptism a symbolic doorway to a new kind of life, through which He would be the first to walk.[54]

When Jesus approached John for baptism, John declared that it was he that needed to be baptized by Jesus. John understood his ministry to be the forerunner of the Messiah and recognized Jesus' righteousness and holiness, Matthew 3:11-12. However, Jesus insisted upon John performing the rite of baptism stating, "Suffer it to be so now: for thus it becometh us to fulfill all righteousness" (Matthew 3:15). Jesus Christ had come to fulfill every aspect of God's law and present Himself as the righteous One without fault or sin. Jesus later proclaimed, "Think not that I am come to destroy the law, or the prophets: I am not come to destroy, but to fulfill" (Matthew 5:17). Upon completion of Jesus' baptism, the three synoptic gospels record the recognition of Jesus by the Heavenly Father. "And lo a voice from heaven, saying, This is my beloved Son, in whom I am well pleased" (Matthew 3:17).

It was also at Jesus' baptism that John acknowledged Jesus as the "Lamb of God, which taketh away the sin of the world" (John 1:29). This identification carries so many spiritual implications. John acknowledged Jesus as being the Lamb that God had promised to provide to be man's substitutionary sacrifice. Jesus came not to simply atone or cover man's

---

[54] Charles R. Swindoll, *The Greatest Life of All: Jesus*, 52.

sin; but, to take it away once and for all. The Lamb was provided for the suffering and payment for sin. The Lamb would shed His blood and die. The redemption of God was offered for all the world. Jesus came to address the real and primary need of Israel and all of mankind—sin!

As prophesied centuries earlier by the prophet Isaiah, Jesus was anointed by the Spirit of God. "And the spirit of the LORD shall rest upon him, the spirit of wisdom and understanding, the spirit of counsel and might, the spirit of knowledge and of the fear of the LORD" (Isaiah 11:2) (cf. Isaiah 42:1; 61:1). Peter, after the crucifixion and ascension of Jesus Christ, communicated an inspired testimony of the ministry of Jesus. Peter spoke of "How God anointed Jesus of Nazareth with the Holy Ghost and with power: who went about doing good, and healing all that were oppressed of the devil; for God was with him" (Acts 10:38). The incarnate Christ chose to accomplish His mission and ministry through the power of the Holy Spirit of God. By doing this, Jesus became the example to future believers that the work of God would be accomplished through those who surrendered themselves to the Holy Spirit of God.

It was the Spirit of God, according to Matthew 4:1-11, who led Jesus into the wilderness to face the temptations of Satan. Jesus spent forty days fasting in the wilderness and endured and resisted temptations in every category. In 1 John 2:16, Scriptures identify these categories as the "lust of the eyes, lust of the flesh, and the pride of life". Ryrie notes the following perspective concerning the temptation of Jesus:

> Satan's intention in the temptation was to make Christ sin so as to thwart God's plan for man's redemption by disqualifying the Savior. God's purpose (note that the Spirit led Jesus to the test) was to prove His Son to be sinless and thus a worthy Savior. It is clear that He actually was tempted; it is equally clear that He was sinless (2 Cor. 5:21).[55]

---

[55] Charles Ryrie, *Ryrie Study Bible, King James Version*, 1421. Notes on Matthew 4:1.

The three categories in which Jesus was tempted and successfully resisted were the same three areas in which Adam and Eve were tempted and failed. Jesus is identified as the *last Adam* and *second Man* in 1 Corinthians 15:45-49. The first Adam encountered Satan in the Garden, visibly and physically, and succumbed to temptation. The second Adam confronted Satan in the wilderness, visibly and physically, and defeated the enemy of God and man. However, this was only the beginning of Satan's attempts to thwart the plan of God!

Jesus came as God-Man to restore what was lost through the disobedience and sin of Adam. It was through sinful Adam that all men had sin imputed unto them and were separated from God. It would be through the sinless Jesus Christ, 'God's Lamb', that all men could have righteousness imputed unto them and be reconciled to God!

Immediately following His wilderness experience, Jesus began calling several men to become His disciples and follow Him. This intimate relationship would allow Jesus to teach and train these men in the ways of God. It would be Christ's disciples who would continue His ministry of reconciliation after He had ascended back to His Father. With these twelve chosen men, Jesus launched His itinerant preaching ministry throughout the Galilean and Judean countryside.

The message Jesus Christ proclaimed to the people was revolutionary and contradictory to the teaching of the rabbis of Israel. The rabbis basically instructed the people to strictly observe the Mosaic Law and the Talmud. The Talmud is the collection of Jewish law and the traditional teachings of various rabbis. The instructions promoted that through the individual's efforts one could become good and righteous enough to obtain God's favor. Jesus, however, called people to repent of their sin and acknowledge the holiness of God. Christ addressed the issues of the heart of man and stressed that man's heart needed to be changed before the actions, or lives, of men would change for righteousness. "For out of the heart proceed evil thoughts, murders, adulteries, fornications, thefts, false witness, blasphemies: These are the things which defile a man:" (Matthew 15:19-20a). Jesus illustrated the inner working of God within the life and heart of man with the picturesque language describing the cleaning of a cup and plate. "Woe unto you, scribes and Pharisees, hypocrites! for ye make the outside of the cup and of the platter, but within they are full of extortion and excess. Thou blind Pharisee, cleanse first that which is within the cup and platter, that the outside of them may be clean also" (Matthew 23:25-26).

Jesus called the people to return to the unadulterated Scripture, over the traditions of men. The accusation of being hypocrites was levied against the Pharisees and teachers of Israel. Jesus rebuked these teachers of the law by reminding them of Isaiah's prophecy: "This people draweth nigh unto me with their mouth, and honoureth me with their lips; but their heart is far from me. But in vain they do worship me, teaching for doctrines the commandments of men" (Matthew 15:8-9). "Jesus didn't come to earth to establish a new religion. He came to restore a broken relationship. He came to make the primary, primary again. The secondary activity of obedience to the law of God was always intended to serve the primary activity: to love God and enjoy Him forever."[56]

Struggling to comprehend this new kind of life Jesus was offering, Nicodemus, Israel's leading theologian, sought out Jesus and asked for explanation. The discourse between Nicodemus and Jesus took a completely foreign approach than Nicodemus anticipated. Jesus told Nicodemus this new life began with a new birth! Nicodemus was directed to a relationship with God through faith in the sacrificial work of redemption in which Jesus came to fulfill, John 3:1-21. Nicodemus was reminded of a biblical account, Numbers 21:4-9, within Israel's history that illustrated this work of faith to acquire spiritual healing. Jesus reminded Nicodemus, "And as Moses lifted up the serpent in the wilderness, even so must the Son of man be lifted up: That whosoever believeth in him should not perish, but have eternal life" (John 3:14-15). This act of Moses in the desert was definitely a foreshadow of Jesus being judged for the sin of man on the cross.

The teaching of Jesus took the law of God to a new level. He spoke of taking the letter of the law and adding to it the appropriate motive, or inner heart. This is seen throughout the greatest sermon ever recorded that was spoken by Man. In what has been entitled as the Sermon on

---

[56] Charles R. Swindoll, *The Greatest Life of All: Jesus*, 84.

the Mount, Matthew 5-7, Jesus began with the instruction of the law, i.e., "Ye have heard that it was said ... ", and expounded it further by adding, "But I say unto you ... " The truths that Jesus taught the people began to produce a strong following. There were some who recognized Jesus' teaching as surpassing that of Israel's teachers."For he taught them as one having authority, and not as the scribes" (Matthew 7:29).

The religious teachers were very concerned that Jesus was attempting to destroy and negate the law of God. They approached Jesus attempting to obtain a charge against Him to enable them to legally expose Jesus as a blasphemer and discredit Him to the people. A lawyer posed to Jesus this question, "Master, which is the great commandment in the law?" Jesus' response was engraved with wisdom as He summed up the multitude of commands into two. "Jesus said unto him, Thou shalt love the Lord thy God with all thy heart, and with all thy soul, and with all thy mind. This is the first and great commandment. And the second is like unto it, Thou shalt love thy neighbor as thyself. On these two commandments hang all the law and the prophets" (Matthew 22:36-40).

Throughout the preaching and teaching ministry of Jesus, those who opposed Him continued to attempt to trap Him in some false teaching. The enemies of Christ were unsuccessful in finding any blasphemous teaching within the doctrine of Jesus. "And no man was able to answer him a word, neither durst any man from that day forth ask him any more questions" (Matthew 22:46). Thus, 'God's Lamb' was pure and infallible in His teaching. There were no contradictions found in His teaching; He spoke only the truth!

As Jesus' teaching was public, so was His life. The scrutiny of today's politicians and public figures pale in comparison to the intense and meticulous scrutiny of Jesus' life and ministry. Everything He did, everything He said, everything He touched, everywhere He went, and everyone He interacted with came under the watchful eye of the religious and political leaders of His day. Throughout the three and one-half years of His public ministry, the enemies of Jesus constantly looked for a blemish in His character. They never found any 'skeletons' in Jesus' closet! His life was as transparent and pure as crystal.

There was no prejudice with Jesus and He was no respecter of persons. Jesus Christ, the 'Lamb of God', had come to redeem people from all ethnic groups, all walks of life, all nationalities, every economic status, and all age groups. Jesus came to extend God's grace, forgive sin, and save all who would trust in Him!

To the sanctimoniously religious, Jesus admonished to repent of their religiosity and turn to a personal relationship with God by faith in the Son of God, as already observed in the life of Nicodemus, John 3. In contrast to the esteemed Nicodemus was Levi, who is the same as Matthew.

Matthew's occupation was the most repulsive and despised trades in which a Jew could be employed. He was a tax collector for the Romans. Tax collectors had a bad reputation for malpractice and extortion. They were not to be associated with or to be trusted. Yet, Jesus approached Matthew and not only forgave him of his sin, but called him to be one of His twelve disciples. Matthew immediately held a celebration to commemorate his salvation and call to service. Of course, the only friends Matthew had to invite were other tax collectors and publicans. Publicans were individuals whose occupations rendered them ceremonially unclean in the eyes of the self-righteous Pharisees. Therefore, anyone who associated with the publicans who were recognized as sinners, was also rendered ceremonially unclean. However, Jesus accepted Matthew's invitation to his celebratory dinner. When the Pharisees challenged Jesus about this, His reply was declarative of His mission. "But when Jesus heard that, he said unto them, They that be whole need not a physician, but they that be sick. But go ye and learn what that meaneth, I will have mercy, and not sacrifice: For I am not come to call the righteous, but sinners to repentance" (Matthew 9:12-13).

In Luke 5:17-26, an encounter is recorded between Jesus and a paralytic that reveals the power and authority of Jesus to forgive sin. One day when Jesus was in the town of Capernaum, He was teaching a group of people that included Pharisees and doctors of the law. The house in which Jesus was not specifically identified, but could have possibly belonged to His disciple, Peter, Matthew 8:5, 14; Mark 2:1-12.

As the crowd listened intently to Jesus' teaching, four men longed to bring their paralytic friend to Jesus to be healed. Unable to push through the crowd, these four men devised another plan to get before Jesus. They would climb the outside stairs to the clay roof top, dig through the roof above where Jesus sat teaching, and lower their friend in front of the famed healer. Upon seeing the paralytic being lowered before Him, Jesus spoke words unexpected. Instead of speaking words addressing the man's illness, Jesus addressed his sin. "And when he saw their faith, he said unto him, Man, thy sins are forgiven thee" (Luke 5:20). Jesus is always concerned more with the spiritual needs, rather than the physical needs. Jesus' words at once aroused the anger and provoked accusations of blasphemy from the Pharisees. The Pharisees questioned, "Who is this which speaketh blasphemies? Who can forgive sins, but God alone?" (Luke 5:21). Jesus used this occasion to teach a great and powerful truth. He answered their questions with a question and a miracle. He asked, "Whether is easier, to say, Thy sins be forgiven thee; or to say, Rise up and walk? But that ye may know that the Son of man hath power upon earth to forgive sins, (he saith unto the sick of the palsy,) I say unto thee, Arise, and take up thy couch, and go into thine house. And immediately he rose up before them, and took up that whereon he lay, and departed to his own house, glorifying God" (Luke 5:23-25). The crowd stood amazed and gave glory to God for the miracle they had just witnessed. Realizing Jesus had demonstrated His power and authority to forgive sin in answer to the Pharisees' question that only God could forgive sins, the people were gripped with fear. The accusers of Jesus stood bewildered and speechless, unable to respond to this obvious miracle. They had no other choice but to acknowledge that Jesus, the God-Man, could forgive sin!

The apostle John records an encounter between Jesus and a woman in which Jesus extended forgiveness and promoted righteous living. In John 8:1-12, Scriptures provide details of an incident in which the religious leaders brought before Jesus a woman caught in adultery. According to the Mosaic Law, the adulterer and adulteress could legally be stoned to death, Leviticus 20:10. Realizing these self-righteous men were only looking to entrap Him, Jesus used this opportunity to, once again, teach an important lesson. Jesus challenged the woman's accusers, "He that is without sin among you, let him first cast a stone at her" (John 8:7b). This wrought conviction within the hearts of the accusers and resulted in compassion and mercy. All the woman's accusers left without incident. At this, Jesus questioned, "Woman, where are those thine accusers? hath no man condemned thee?" To which the woman responded, "No man, Lord." As the woman acknowledged Jesus as Lord, "Jesus said unto her, Neither do I condemn thee: go, and sin no more" (John 8:10-11). Jesus mercifully offered forgiveness to the repentant woman and admonished her to "sin no more". Jesus not only promoted righteous living, but informed all how it could be accomplished. Jesus said, "I am the light of the world: he that followeth me shall not walk in darkness, but shall have the light of life" (John 8:12).

One of the most powerful miracles that spoke of Jesus' power and authority to give eternal life to those who trust in Him was the resurrection of Lazarus, John 11:1-44. Lazarus, who had died, was a believer of, and a follower of, Jesus Christ. Lazarus had been four days in the tomb when Jesus came to his home in Bethany. While comforting the sisters of Lazarus, Jesus voiced the clearest and most powerful declaration of His power over death and of being the Giver of Life. Jesus said to Martha, "I am the resurrection, and the life: he that believeth in me, though he were dead, yet shall he live:" (John 11:25). Moments later, Jesus commanded the stone be rolled away from the tomb's entrance. When the tomb was opened, Jesus spoke three powerful words, "Lazarus, come forth." To the amazement of all that were present, the process of decomposition was reversed, life was given back to the body of Lazarus, and he stepped forth, grave clothes and all!

The resurrection of Lazarus from the dead enraged the enemies of Jesus. These envious religious leaders realized Jesus was acquiring more and more followers; jeopardizing their influence and authority over the people. It was at this time, Jesus' enemies began to conspire on how they could kill Jesus and remove Him from the scene, John 11:45-54.

All of Jesus' life and ministry was lived in total submission and obedience to the will of the Father! Everything Jesus said, every truth He taught, every miracle He performed, was just as the Heavenly Father wanted. Jesus said, "For I came from heaven, not to do mine own will, but the will of him who sent me. And this is the Father's will which hath sent me, that of all which he hath given me I should lose nothing, but should raise it up again at the last day. And this is the will of him that sent me, that every one which seeth the Son, and believeth on him, may have everlasting life: and I will raise him up at the last day" (John 6:38-40).

Throughout the life and ministry of Jesus Christ, He was meticulously examined and came under the intense scrutiny of the religious leaders of His day. As foreshadowed in the sacrificial system described in Leviticus 22:17-33, the priest's responsibility was to inspect every animal offered for sacrifice. If any blemish was discovered, the animal was immediately disqualified. The sacrificial animal must be perfect and without blemish! "Now the chief priests, and elders, and all the council, sought false witnesses against Jesus, to put him to death; But found none: yea, though many false witnesses came, yet they found none" (Matthew 26:59-60). 'God's Lamb' passed the scrutiny of the priests and was found without fault! Jesus also passed the intense interrogation of the political leaders. Pilate, the Roman Governor, testified of Jesus three different times, "I find no fault in him" (John 18:38; 19:4, 6). Jesus, and He alone, met the requirements to be the ultimate sacrificial Lamb for the redemption of man! 'God's Lamb' had passed inspection! God's plan of redemption was about to come to fruition through the 'Omega Lamb'!

Note the following observations of how Jesus Christ fulfilled the requirements of the acceptable substitutionary sacrifice for man:

1) Jesus Christ was born of a virgin as the God-Man. He was completely innocent and sinless. He was the best God could offer. Genesis 3:15; Isaiah 7:14; Luke 1:26-38.

2) Jesus Christ, completely devoted to the Father, fulfilled every demand of the law of God thereby identifying Himself as the only righteous and perfect Man. Leviticus 2:1-16; Matthew 5:17.

3) Jesus Christ was identified as the promised 'Lamb of God'. Genesis 22:8; John 1:29.

4) Jesus faced and resisted the temptations of Satan. He was tempted in every area, but was without sin. He became our Faithful High Priest, understanding our struggles and successfully interceding for us. Leviticus 2:1-16; Matthew 4:1-11; Hebrews 4:14-16; 7:24-25.

5) Jesus Christ's preaching and teaching promoted repentance within the people and encouraged a right relationship with God. He rebuked and reprimanded the cold religiosity of the teachers of Israel. Leviticus 3:1-17; Isaiah 61:1-2a; Matthew 4:17; Matthew15:19-20; 23:1-28.

6) Jesus Christ's interaction with all people was without prejudice, motivated by divine love, and covered with amazing grace. He promoted reconciliation to God, offered forgiveness, exemplified righteousness, and gave eternal life. Deuteronomy 10:12-20; Isaiah 49:1-6; Luke 5:17-26; John 8:3-12; John 11:1-44.

7) Jesus Christ, 'God's Lamb', passed the meticulous scrutiny of the religious and political leaders. They were unsuccessful in discovering any blemish or fault that would discredit Him from becoming the acceptable sacrifice for the sin of man. Leviticus 22:17-33; Matthew 26:59-60; John 18:38; 19:4, 6.

Even though none of the charges against Jesus could be substantiated, He was about to enter into the mock trial of all ages. Jesus had been accused of blasphemy, by teaching heresy against the Law of God and claiming Himself, a man, to be God! The envy and hatred of the unbelieving religious leaders fueled their resolve to have Jesus discredited and executed. They desired to defame His name, dissolve His influence with the Jewish populace, and dishonor and humiliate His person before all the world!

As previously quoted, Galatians 4:4-5, God sent His virgin born Son, Jesus, to redeem them who were under the penalty of the Law, that all might be reconciled to Holy God and receive the adoption as His children. What the Jewish rabbis failed to recognize, was that the Law's purpose was to bring people to the acknowledgement of their sin, God's holiness, and their need for God's forgiveness through Christ Jesus, 'God's Lamb'. "Wherefore the law was our schoolmaster to bring us unto Christ, that we might be justified by faith" (Galatians 3:24).

'God's Lamb' now faces the most intense trial of His love and devotion for His Father and His love for His creation—man. Jesus Christ will submit Himself to become the supreme sacrifice and shed His innocent and pure blood for the payment of man's sin, once and for all! The blood stained crimson path is about to become a crimson river which overflows with the unblemished blood of the 'Omega Lamb'!

CHAPTER SEVEN

Omega Lamb

Our journey down the crimson path leads to the darkest and most dismal day in the history of man. It was the day the inner most being of man was revealed as black as the darkest night. Man is inherently evil! Man's sinful, depraved, and degenerate nature stood in defiance of God's offer of redemption. This was a desolate day when man spurned the love and grace that the Almighty Creator extended to humanity in the Person—Jesus Christ. The betrayal and crucifixion of Jesus was a wicked and atrocious deed. Yet, it did not take omniscient God by surprise. During this bleakest of days, the love and grace of Holy God shone bright! It was through Jesus Christ all the *foreshadows* of redemption would ultimately find *fulfillment*. The fullness of time had come for God to fulfill His promise and provide the Redeemer. The 'Omega Lamb' (last) would become the supreme sacrifice, once and for all, and through whose blood would be sufficient to save all who trust in Him! Through Jesus Christ, "we are sanctified through the offering of the body of Jesus Christ once for all … he had offered one sacrifice for sins forever, sat down at the right hand of God" (Hebrews 10:10, 12). What does it mean to be 'saved'? What are the ramifications of the phrase 'Jesus saves'? This chapter will examine the various attributes of the salvation provided for each believer in the 'Omega Lamb'—Jesus Christ.

Jesus had been challenged, examined, and interrogated throughout His entire ministry. His opposition remained unable to expose Him as a false prophet or a deceiver. The fame of Jesus birthed envy within the religious leaders and they adamantly refused to surrender their political power and popular influence. Fueled by their envious hatred, the enemies of Jesus combined forces to plot His demise. Due to Jesus' popularity, He was untouchable in public. A sinister plan began to evolve to arrest Jesus in the darkness of night when the crowds had dispersed to their homes. The opportunity was presented from a most unlikely place.

One of Jesus' own disciples, Judas Iscariot, had misunderstood Jesus' mission and had become disillusioned with Jesus. Judas concluded that Jesus did not fit his predetermined image of Israel's Messiah, for Jesus had not made any attempt to recruit an army by which to deliver Israel from her oppression. The week prior to His crucifixion, though Jesus had entered into Jerusalem riding upon a donkey, He was hailed by the crowds as Messiah. Judas realized that Jesus' popularity had reached its all time high, but he witnessed Him deliberately forfeiting the best opportunity to claim the position of King of the Jews and the throne of David. Judas responded by consorting with the chief rulers that for the price of a common slave (thirty pieces of silver), he would stealthily deliver Jesus into their hands.

There was an underlying battle ensuing: the war between good and evil; between God and Satan. The spiritual warfare was becoming more intense. Two gospel writers, John and Luke, wrote that Satan entered Judas and beguiled him to betray Jesus into the hands of His enemies, Luke 22:3 and John 13:2, 27. Throughout Jesus' life on earth, Satan continuously attempted to thwart God's plan of redemption for man. Satan may have thought he had finally gained the upper hand through Judas Iscariot.

In the dead of night, Judas betrayed Jesus and led His accusers to falsely arrest Him at the secluded garden Jesus regularly visited for a time of prayer. Jesus was immediately taken into the presence of Annas, a former High Priest, for the first of six illegal trials. By the early dawning of the next day, Jesus would endure three illegal Jewish and religious trials and three illegal Roman civil trails. Illegal, because the trials were initiated during the cover of the darkness of the night and all allegations levied against Jesus were false and unsubstantiated. Herein is truth revealed as the Scriptures proclaim—that men loved darkness because their deeds were evil, John 3:19-20. The innocent Son of God, Jesus, could have called upon heaven's angels to free Him from His captors, but refused for He knew this was the plan of God unfolding. Jesus could have argued and presented truth to prove His innocence, but He remained silent. "Jesus recognized a basic fact of life: words are wasted on people who have no desire for truth."[57] Therefore, as a lamb led to the slaughter, the One that John the Baptist had identified as the 'Lamb of God' opened not His mouth in His defense, or in retaliation.

The religious leaders had begun to understand the significance of Jesus' ministry and recognized His identity as Messiah. Jesus had clearly revealed Himself to them as Messiah on several occasions, John 5:18; 7:25-30; 10:21-33; Mark 14:61-62; Matthew 26:63-64; Luke 22:70. However, they refused to accept His Messiahship as it would depreciate their position and affluence. These leaders wanted a militant King that would promote them, not a suffering Savior to die for them!

Scriptures reveal that Pilate, the Roman procurator, knew that envy motivated the religious leaders to arrest Jesus and to manipulate His death, Matthew 27:18. Even Herod, the Roman appointed puppet King of the Jews, found nothing of which to accuse Jesus of, Luke 23:6-12. Although Pilate was unsuccessful in finding fault in Jesus, especially any fault worthy of death, he resigned to the Sanhedrin's argument and relinquished the innocent Jesus to the executioners for crucifixion.

The rugged and war hardened soldiers made sport of and tortured Jesus through verbal and physical abuse. Jesus was severely scourged nearly beyond recognition. Mockingly, they placed a purple robe on Jesus' badly beaten and bloodied body and pressed upon His head a crown of thorns. Adding to His humiliation, the soldiers smote Jesus with their fists, spat upon Him, and mocked His prophetic abilities.

---

[57] Charles R. Swindoll, *The Greatest Life of All: Jesus* (Nashville, Tennessee: Thomas Nelson, Inc., 2008), 208.

Afterwards, they stripped Him of the robe, replacing it with His bloody and torn clothing, and led Him to His death. Jesus Christ began His painful and horrific journey to Golgotha, carrying the rugged wooden cross upon which He would be unmercifully crucified.

Grotesquely beaten and nailed to a cross, Jesus hung suspended between heaven and earth; His precious, sinless blood spilling from His body. In naked shame and humiliation, Jesus suffered intense and excruciating physical pain. For three hours (nine that morning to noon), the crowd mocked and jeered at His agony; soldiers gambled for the clothes of the crucified; and the religious leaders issued a final challenge to Jesus to prove Himself to be the Messiah and remove Himself from the cross.

At high noon, an ominous darkness covered the land! For the next three hours, the darkness concealed from the unbelieving glare of Jesus' accusers His most horrendous suffering. The people surrounding the cross heard Jesus cry out, "My God, my God, why hast thou forsaken me?" (Matthew 27:46). Jesus began to suffer as never before as Holy God began to pour out the wrath upon Him for the sin of mankind. For the first time in eternity, Jesus, the sinless Son of God, felt the deadly sting of sin as He became sin for man. As the 'Omega Lamb', Jesus came not to *cover* man's sin, but to *take away* the sin. Jesus purchased our redemption " ... with the precious blood of Christ, as a lamb without blemish and without spot" (1 Peter 1:19). At around three in the afternoon, Jesus spoke His last, but powerful words: *It is finished*! (John 19:30); Jesus then died. Jesus died on the day of preparation of the Passover and at the time the Passover lambs were sacrificed. All that was needed to be accomplished for man's redemption from sin, deliverance from the oppression of Satan, and reconciliation to God had been done! Christ is our Passover!

Though the soldiers led Jesus to His crucifixion, they and the people calling for His death failed to recognize Jesus was voluntarily and lovingly giving Himself to be shamed, humiliated, beaten, and crucified as man's substitute. Jesus made this truth clear in His teaching as recorded in the tenth chapter of John. "I am the good shepherd: the good shepherd giveth his life for the sheep" (John 10:11); " ... I lay down my life for the sheep" (John 10:15b); " … I lay down my life, that I might take it again. No man taketh it from me, but I lay it down of myself. I have power to lay it down, and I have power to take it again. This commandment have I received from my Father" (John 10:17b-18). Again, Jesus' words in Matthew 20:28 reveal this truth, "Even as the Son of man came not to be ministered unto, but to minister, and give his life a ransom for many." Jesus came to die for the sin of mankind! He came knowing His destiny was the cross!

One may still question the need for Jesus Christ to die and why the need for the shedding of blood. A very important lesson to be learned from the offerings of Cain and Abel is that man must approach God in the way He prescribed. Fruchtenbaum provides this insight:

> If there is one theme that seems to go throughout the entire Scriptures, it is the theme of redemption by blood … One cannot approach God by whatever means one chooses. It is man who sinned and offended the holy God; it is God who must do the forgiving. Therefore, it is not for man to choose the means of forgiveness but for God, and God has chosen the means to be blood.[58]

The Scriptures corroborate this truth, " … the blood of Jesus Christ his Son cleanseth us from all sin" (1 John 1:7b).

What is involved in the salvation that Jesus provides? What did Jesus accomplish for us through His death? What does the Bible say that those who, in faith, trust Jesus as Savior and Lord receive? What are the benefits of becoming a follower of Jesus Christ, a Christian?

First and foremost, there is nothing else needed to be done for salvation and forgiveness of sin! When Jesus cried out, "It is finished", the price of man's redemption was paid in full. The Bible reveals the price of one's sin is death and that Jesus died a vicarious and substitutionary death for sinners. One's redemption does not rest upon one's accomplishments, but on what Jesus accomplished! Unlike

---

[58] Arnold G. Fruchtenbaum *Messianic Christology* (San Antonio, Texas: Ariel Ministries, 1998), 129.

the Levivtical sacrifices that needed to be repeated continuously and annually on the Day of Atonement, the one-time sacrifice Jesus offered was sufficient for all and for all time. The writer of Hebrews provides this insightful truth, "Neither by the blood of goats and calves, but by his own blood he entered in once into the holy place, having obtained eternal redemption for us ... once in the end of the world hath he appeared to put away sin by the sacrifice of himself" (Hebrews 9:12 and 26b).

As the high Priest, by the blood sacrifice of a lamb, once a year entered into the Holy of Holies within the earthly tabernacle, Jesus Christ entered once for all time into the heavenly Holy of Holies by His own blood and became the eternal High Priest, Hebrews 9:11-12. This eliminated the need for further sacrifices for sin. The innocent God-Man became the substitute for guilty-man! The writer of Hebrews wrote that Jesus, " ... by the grace of God should taste death for every man" (Hebrews 2:9). God's forgiveness of one's sin is based upon the shed blood of the 'Omega Lamb'—Jesus Christ!

What does it mean to be forgiven of one's sin? God can forgive one's sin because He paid the penalty for sin. God is a holy and righteous judge. He is not moved with sympathy and sentiment to exclude His justice and righteousness toward sin. The righteousness of God demands that sin's penalty be paid. Only then can forgiveness be extended. McGee wrote, "Christ's death and the shedding of His blood is the foundation for forgiveness and, without that, there could be no forgiveness."[59] The beauty of God's forgiveness is that He can do what no human can do— forgive and forget! No one will be liable for sin that has been forgiven and cleansed by the blood of the 'Omega Lamb'! Forgiven sin will never be remembered by God. "And their sins and iniquities will I remember no more" (Hebrews 10:17). Praise God! All because of the 'Lamb of God' that takes away the sin of the world!

Another benefit of redemption through the 'Omega Lamb' is that He provides the acceptable covering through which one can approach

---

[59] J. Vernon McGee, *Thru The Bible, Vol. V* (Nashville, Tennessee: Thomas Nelson Publishers, 1981), 220.

Holy God. Jesus died in naked shame so that believers could be clothed in His righteousness—unashamed. When Adam and Eve sinned, they lost their covering of 'light'. When one trusts Jesus as Savior, the Holy Spirit indwells the believer and imputes to him the righteousness of Jesus. Jesus declared that He was the "light of the world" (John 8:12). When Holy God looks at a believer in Jesus, He sees the righteousness of Jesus and not the sinner. Thus, the believer can now enter boldly into God's presence and " … obtain mercy, and find grace to help in time of need" (Hebrews 4:15-16). The shed blood of Jesus acquired access to the Father for all believers. The veil of the Temple was torn from top to bottom allowing entrance to all who would come to the Father through Jesus.

Another attribute of salvation in Jesus is the eternal redemption for all who trust in Him. To redeem something is to pay the price for that object. The Bible declares the price of sin is death, but that the gift of God is eternal life, Romans 6:23. One's salvation has been purchased by God through Jesus Christ and offered as a free gift to man through faith in Christ. Ephesians 2:8-9 states that one is saved by the grace of God and not by any works in which one could accomplish. In fact, Isaiah stated that a man's most righteous works were nothing more than filthy rags in the sight of Holy God, Isaiah 64:6. This affirms that one cannot merit God's forgiveness and salvation simply by living a good life, or a life characterized by good works. The Bible continuously points to the shed blood of Jesus Christ as the source for one's redemption and by which one receives the forgiveness of sin, Ephesians 1:7. Interestingly, the Greek word used and translated as redemption in Ephesians 1:7, is 'apolutrosis'; that carries the meaning of "liberation from the guilt and doom of sin and the introduction into a life of liberty."[60] In Christ, one is no longer under the weight and penalty of sin and is set free from the bondage of sin. One is then free to experience the new life in Christ, Romans 6:4. The adage that there are many ways to heaven is untrue! The Bible declares that the only way into heaven is through faith and

---

[60] William E. Vine, *An Expository Dictionary of New Testament Words* (Old Tappan, New Jersey: Fleming H. Revell Company, 1940, Seventeenth impression, 1966), 264.

trust in Jesus Christ alone, John 14:6. Although this sounds intolerant, it is a great truth—one simply needs to trust in Jesus to be saved!

Saved from what? Saved from the wrath of God against sin! This truth was illustrated in the Book of Exodus through the 'Paschal (Passover) Lamb'. It was the applied blood of the lamb that caused the Lord to pass over the house and spare the inhabitants His judgment and wrath against sin. When the precious blood of the 'Omega Lamb', Jesus Christ, is applied to the heart of the individual, the believer is spared the coming judgment and wrath of Holy God. The Bible speaks much of the wrath of God and His wrath finds fruition in the unbeliever spending eternity in hell, the eternal lake of fire! The Bible reveals that hell was initially designed as a place for the devil and his angels, Matthew 25:41. John, the writer of Revelation, prophetically tells of the day in which the devil, his angels, and all unbelieving Christ rejecters shall be cast into hell to be tormented for eternity, Revelation 20:10, 14-15. However, all believers, " ... being now justified by his blood, we shall be saved from wrath through him" (Romans 5:9). Jesus suffered the wrath of God that believers might be spared!

A believer in Jesus Christ is saved from the oppression of Satan. Again, illustrated through the Passover experience, the Israelites were instructed to partake of the Passover meal fully and completely dressed and packed to leave Egypt. When the judgment of God was inflicted upon Egypt, Pharaoh immediately forced the Hebrews out of the land. Due to the implementation of the blood of the 'Paschal Lamb', the Israelites were freed from slavery, dominion, and the severe oppression of the Egyptians! This was a foreshadow of the work of the 'Omega Lamb' to deliver the sinner from the slavery, dominion, and oppression of sin. "For this purpose the Son of God was manifested, that he might destroy the works of the devil" (1 John 3:8b). As one surrenders to Christ Jesus, sin will not have dominion, Romans 6:14. One is encouraged and challenged to continue in the liberty and freedom in Christ, refusing to become entangled in that which would result in bondage, Galatians 5:1. Prior to Jesus in one's life as Savior, one is enslaved to sin without option. After one's salvation experience, one has a choice. Scriptures reveal in the sixth chapter of Romans that a believer has the option of whom he will serve—sin, self, and unrighteousness, or Jesus and righteousness. Jesus Christ removes the penalty of sin for every believer. A life of surrender and obedience to Jesus Christ after salvation will eliminate the guilt and condemnation of sin. Herein lies the importance of choosing to live in obedience to Christ: "There is therefore now no condemnation to them which are in Christ Jesus, who walk not after the flesh, but after the Spirit" (Romans 8:1).

Another wondrous benefit of trusting Jesus Christ as Savior and Lord is that the believer becomes a Child of God. This results in the believer receiving from God everything that is needed to live a godly life and the gracious benefit of the believer becoming a partaker of God's divine nature, 2 Peter 1:3-4. In Galatians 4:5, the Scripture reveals this great purpose of the redemption God offers through Jesus Christ. Jesus came, "To redeem them that were under the law, that we might receive the adoption of sons." This truth correlates with what Jesus told Nicodemus in the third chapter of John; a person must be born again. When one receives the adoption into the family of God, one receives position and privilege. Through faith in Christ, one is born into the family of God as a newborn babe. This position necessitates one's growth and development in grace through the ingestion and application of the Word of God, 1 Peter 2:2. Simultaneously, by the act of God, one is adopted into the family of God as a full grown child. This provides one with the rights and privileges of one's new family of God. An adopted child becomes legally entitled to the property, rights, and status of the adopter. An individual that has been saved for a length of time has no more advantage in understanding the Scriptures than a new born Child of God. It is the same Holy Spirit who teaches and enables one to understand the word of God. In Romans 8:14-17, one is taught that the indwelling Holy Spirit gives witness to our relationship with God. It is through this relationship one is delivered from the bondage of sin and fear and is drawn into a close intimacy with God, whereby the child can call God, *Abba* Father. "*Abba* is a very personal word that could be translated "My Daddy." We don't use this word in reference to

God because of the danger of becoming overly familiar with Him. But it expresses a heart-cry, especially in times of trouble."[61]

Through the adoption into the family of God, one finds the foundation of the assurance of one's salvation. Jesus taught that the Holy Spirit of God would dwell *with* each believer and dwell *inside* each believer, John 14:17. Jesus also taught that He and the Father would make their home within each believer, John 14:23. This is definitely above one's comprehension of how the Triune Godhead could reside within each individual believer! However, this is a great truth! The Scriptures further teach that God will never leave or forsake a believer, Hebrews 13:5. An even stronger truth that provides assurance of one's salvation and relationship with God is found in 2 Timothy 2:13. "If we are faithless, He remains faithful: He cannot deny Himself."[62] Therefore, if the Father, the Son, and the Holy Spirit lives within, God is faithful always, and will never, *cannot* ever, deny His child! If He did, God would be denying Himself! One's salvation originates and is sustained by the Lord. Concerning 2 Timothy 2:13, Ryrie offers his insight: "A statement of the consistency of God's character, a strong promise to the believer of the security of his salvation even though he may lose all rewards."[63]

Another work of salvation within the life of the believer is that God makes the believer into a new creation! When a sinner repents of sin and trusts Jesus as Savior, the Holy Spirit indwells the individual. When Holy God enters into the life of a sinner, things change! If there has been no change in one's life and behavior since one claimed to be saved, then there has been no salvation! One reads in 2 Corinthians 5:17, "Therefore if any man be in Christ, he is a new creature: old things are passed away; behold, all things are become new." If one has no problem continuing in a sinful lifestyle—no salvation!

---

[61] J. Vernon McGee, *Thru The Bible, Vol. IV* (Nashville, Tennessee: Thomas Nelson Publishers, 1981), 701

[62] *The Holy Bible, New King James Version* (Nashville, Tennessee: Broadman & Holman Publishers, 1996), 1048.

[63] Charles Ryrie, *Ryrie Study Bible, King James Version* (Chicago, Illinois: Moody Publishers, 1986, 1994), 1836. notes on 2 Timothy 2:13.

Another ceaseless benefit of trusting Jesus Christ as Savior is the eternal life in Him. The question of one's salvation is forever settled in Christ. Jesus pronounced that He was the resurrection and the life, John 11:25. Simply put, Jesus' eternal life will allow believers to live forever with Him! He died that believers in Him might live. "Wherefore he is able also to save them to the uttermost that come to God by him, seeing he ever liveth to make intercession for us" (Hebrews 7:25). The Lord Jesus promised that the Holy Spirit would live within each believer and it is the Holy Spirit who is the guarantee of one's eternal salvation. In Ephesians 1:13-14, one learns that a believer is sealed by the Holy Spirit of promise. This Seal of God cannot be broken by anyone or anything!

The culmination of redemption is that the believer in Jesus Christ receives a great inheritance and is elevated to a royal position. In Romans 8:17, one reads that the child of God becomes a joint heir of Jesus Christ and an heir of God. Wow! Out of His amazing grace, the heavenly Father will reward the believer for something he did not do! All believers will inherit with Christ because they are in Christ, Ephesians 1:11. Amazingly, God's grace does not stop there. Scriptures reveal the redeemed will be elevated to sit in the heavenly places with the Lord Jesus and are promoted to the position of kings and priests, Ephesians 2:6; Revelation 1:6. This is through the grace of God, not our merit!

> God is no respecter of persons. Redemption through the 'Omega Lamb', Jesus Christ, is available to everyone. No one is excluded! Only Jesus Christ, through His death, satisfied the righteous holy wrath of God toward sin. Jesus is the propitiation for sin. Scripture is clear that:
>
> "For all have sinned and come short of the glory of God. Being justified freely by his grace through the redemption that is in Christ Jesus. Whom God hath set forth to be a propitiation through faith in his blood, to declare his righteousness for the remission of sins that are past, through the forbearance of God; to declare, I say, at this time his righteousness: that he might be

just, and the justifier of him which believeth in Jesus"
(Romans 3:23-26).

Jesus died for the sins of the entire world and all of mankind—past,
present, and future! In 1 John 2:2 one reads, "And he is the propitiation
for our sins: and not for ours only, but *for the sins of the whole world*"
(italics mine).

The word 'gospel' means 'good news'. The message for every
individual is " ... that Christ died for our sins according to the
scriptures; And that he was buried, and that he rose again according
to the scriptures" (1 Corinthians 15:3-4). Jesus Christ fulfilled all the
prophecies concerning the work of redemption for man. He died for us,
but He rose the third day and is very much alive today! He is eternal
life! Edersheim expresses the importance of the resurrection of Jesus
Christ: "A dead Christ might have been a Teacher and Wonder-worker,
and remembered as such. But only a Risen and Living Christ could be
the Saviour, the Life, and the Life-Giver—and as such preached to all
men."[64] The resurrection of Jesus Christ proved Him to be the Son of
God, Romans 1:4, and validated everything Jesus said and promised.

The Jewish teachers and rabbis, both ancient and modern, have
always divided the Scriptures into three sections: The Law, The Prophets,
and The Writings. It was to these Scriptures that Jesus Christ directed
His disciples to substantiate His teaching. He never asked His disciples
to simply believe; rather, He directed them to the authority of their own
Scriptures. On the road to Emmaus, the resurrected Christ clearly taught
two of His disciples of the prophetic truth of His sacrificial suffering
and death. As stated in the Gospel According to Luke, Chapter 24:25-
27, 44-48, Jesus Christ began with the writings of Moses, The Law,
and continued through The Prophets and The Writings, teaching the
necessity of His vicarious death. He opened their minds to understand
how He, Messiah, fulfilled all the prophecies of His first coming. Jesus'
disciples came to understand His death and resurrection were in perfect

[64] Alfred Edersheim, *The Life And Times Of Jesus The Messiah* (Peabody, Maine:
Hendrickson Publishers, 1993), Tenth Printing—September 2009. 906.

accordance with the three sections of their authoritative Scripture and essential to prove Him to be the Savior, the Messiah. The Lord Jesus also used the Scriptures to teach His disciples of His second coming. His disciples learned well and used these same Scriptures to prove to both Jews and Gentiles the authenticity of Jesus' Messiahship.

Note the following fulfillments of Jesus Christ being the supreme and ultimate final sacrifice for the sin of man and what He has accomplished for believers:

1) The 'Omega Lamb', Jesus Christ, accomplished everything needed for one's salvation, Genesis 3:15; John 19:30; Hebrews 9:12.

2) It is the blood of Jesus Christ, the 'Omega Lamb', that cleanses one of sin, Leviticus 17:11; 1 John 1:7b.

3) Jesus Christ, 'Omega Lamb', took away sin, John 1:29; Hebrews 9:26.

4) Jesus Christ provided one with the acceptable covering by which to approach Holy God as He exchanged His righteousness for man's sin, Genesis 3:21; Isaiah 61:10; 2 Corinthians 5:21.

5) Through Jesus Christ one will be delivered from the wrath of Holy God, Exodus 12:13, 23; Romans 5:9; 1 Thessalonians 5:9.

6) In Christ, one is set free from the penalty and bondage of sin to experience a new life of liberty in Christ!, Romans 6:4; Galatians 5:1.

7) In Christ, forgiven sin has been forgotten and never remembered, Leviticus 16:8-10, 21-22; Hebrews 10:17.

8) There is no condemnation to those who trust Jesus as Savior and surrender their lives to live for Him, Romans 8:1.

9) In Christ, the believer receives the position and privilege of being adopted into the family of God, Galatians 4:5; Romans 8:15; Ephesians 1:5.

10) Salvation originates and is sustained by God through Jesus Christ. He will never forsake or deny His children. God is always faithful, 2 Timothy 2:13; Hebrews 13:5.

11) The believer in Jesus Christ is eternally secure and sealed by the Holy Spirit who resides within every believer, John 11:25; Ephesians 1:13-14.

12) Through Jesus Christ the believer is created into a new creation, given everything needed for a godly life, and becomes a partaker of God's divine nature, 2 Corinthians 5:17; 2 Peter 1:3-4.

13) Through the grace of God and Jesus Christ, the believer receives an eternal inheritance and is elevated to a royal position, Ephesians 1:11; John 14:1-3; Ephesians 2:6; Revelation 1:6; Romans 8:17.

14) Jesus' sacrifice was the propitiation for the sins of the world, Romans 3:23-26; 1 John 2:2.

15) Jesus Christ rose again the third day and is now Alive!—exalted, extolled, and lifted very high, Isaiah 52:13; Philippians 2:5-11.

Do you desire to know what love looks like? Look at the cross of Jesus Christ! The cross of Jesus Christ testifies to how much God loves every person. To God the word *love* is a verb, not a noun. God *gave* His Son; God *demonstrated* His love to us through Jesus Christ. Do you desire to know what hate looks like? Look at the cross of Jesus Christ! The cross of Jesus Christ testifies to how much God hates sin!

Omega is the last and final letter in the Greek alphabet. Jesus Christ is the 'Omega Lamb'—the ultimate and final sacrifice for sin! There is no other sacrifice sufficient to satisfy the holy wrath of God. In Jesus

Christ, one stands before God justified! To be justified means to be as if one had never sinned! The price of sin has been paid forever and for all. Jesus paid it all!

> Jesus paid it all,
> All to Him I owe;
> Sin had left a crimson stain,
> He washed it white as snow.[65]

The resurrected Jesus Christ spent forty days presenting Himself to various people proving that He did, in fact, rise victorious from the dead. Jesus first appeared to Mary Magdalene and the women that came to the tomb in which His lifeless body had been placed. Graciously, Jesus appeared to Peter first and began a ministry of reconciliation between Him and Peter. Afterward, the resurrected Savior presented Himself to all of the disciples within the locked upper room and on the shore of the Sea of Galilee. At sometime, Jesus appeared to His half-brothers, James and Jude. After which, they became believers and followers of Jesus Christ. According to 1 Corinthians 15:1-11, there were over five hundred at one time who saw the resurrected Christ. Jesus had shown Himself alive " … by many infallible proofs, being seen of them forty days, and speaking of the things pertaining to the kingdom of God" (Acts 1:3).

After the forty days, Jesus led the disciples to the Mount of Olives where He communicated to them His final instructions and promise. He informed them of His departure and ascension back to heaven. They were to remain and continue the work of spreading the gospel message of salvation and redemption to the inhabitants of the world. The disciples were instructed to remain in Jerusalem until they had received from the Heavenly Father the promised empowerment to carry out their ministry.

As Jesus completed delivering His instructions, the Scriptures record His ascension back to His Father. As the disciples were looking

---

[65] Elvina M. Hall, *Jesus Paid It All*. Public domain. *www.library.timelesstruths.org/* accessed July 30, 2014.

at Him and listening to His final words, Jesus began to ascend upward from the ground and continued upward until the clouds hid Him from their sight. Stunned and bewildered, the disciples had failed to see the two angels standing at their side. The angels encouraged these soon-to-be champions of the gospel with the message that this same Jesus would return one day in the same manner in which He departed—in the clouds! Approximately, one hundred and twenty followers of Jesus would spend the next ten days in Jerusalem in diligent and fervent prayer awaiting the promise of the Father.

The journey down the crimson path will now proceed into the heavenly present, as well as the prophesied future. The Book of Revelation will, as Isaiah prophesied, reveal how Jesus Christ, the 'Omega Lamb of God', is now exalted, extolled, and lifted very high. 'Worthy is the Lamb'!

Chapter Eight

Worthy is the Lamb!

The crimson path that wound through the Old Testament foreshadows and into the New Testament fulfillment of these foreshadows in the Person of Jesus Christ progresses now into eternity present and future. Before the journey continues, reflect upon what led to this juncture. Jesus Christ, the 'Lamb of God', has shed His innocent blood, been crucified for man's sin, was buried, and was resurrected on the third day! The glorified Christ ascended from the Mount of Olives and returned to Heaven from whence He came.

In Philippians 2:5-8, the Bible presents the *mind of Christ Jesus* in coming to be man's Redeemer. Before His incarnation, God-the Son was preeminent in Heaven. He was with God; He was God! He displayed all the divine attributes of the Father. The second Person of the Holy Trinity, God-the Son, is equal with God-the Father and enjoyed the elevated positional status of higher than all of the angels. All of Heaven was at His command; ready to do His bidding. It was from this high and superior position, the Son voluntarily and joyfully humbled Himself and stepped down to take the position of a lowly servant.

The mind of Jesus was characterized with " ... lowliness (*humility*), and meekness (*gentleness*), with longsuffering (*patience*), forbearing (*serving*) one another with love" (Ephesians 4:2) (italics mine). Jesus Christ humbled Himself as no one else ever has, or will ever do. Sovereign God took upon Himself the likeness of man and submitted

Himself to the limitations of humanity. He was no less God, though He became wholly man. Why? He did this, motivated by His love, so He could willingly die for the sin of man. Jesus *came* to die! He suffered the death of the cross for all mankind. Jesus was the epitome of Matthew 23:12, "And whosoever shall exalt himself shall be abased (*humbled*); and he that shall humble himself shall be exalted" (italics mine).

Philippians 2:9-11 presents the *mind of God* in His exaltation of Jesus Christ in response to His obedient accomplishment in the redemption of man. Verse nine of the Philippians passage begins with the word, "Wherefore". This word indicates that the following verses present the actions taken by God are due to the preceding actions by Jesus Christ. God-the Father highly exalted Jesus Christ and made the name of Jesus more powerful and prestigious than any other name. Jesus is the only name on which men can call and be saved, Acts 4:12. It is to Jesus that every created being in the universe will bow in reverence and worship; everything in heaven, on earth, and in hell! Jesus Christ is the One that everyone and everything will one day confess as Lord, not as personal Savior, but as Yahweh of the Old Testament, to the glory of God-the Father! This will be elaborated further in the chapter.

Turn to the Book of Revelation and read as John relates the unveiling of Jesus Christ in all His glorious splendor and majesty. It is Jesus Christ who is identified as the One who is, who was, and who is to come; the faithful witness; the first begotten of the dead; the prince of the kings of the earth; and the One who "loved us and washed us from our sin in his own blood" (Revelation 1:4-5). Jesus further identified Himself as the Alpha and Omega, the beginning and the ending, the Almighty. Also in this chapter, Jesus Christ is definitely presented to the reader and described in His glorious, resurrected, and eternal form.

The Apostle John, the writer of the Book of Revelation, was also the disciple who enjoyed the closest and most intimate relationship with the Lord Jesus during His ministry on earth. It was John who leaned toward Jesus at the Last Supper and questioned Jesus as to the identity of His betrayer. John was the only disciple among the twelve that quietly and heartbreakingly observed the final hours of Jesus' agonizing death on the cross. It was to John that Jesus bequeathed the care of His mother, Mary, while He hung suspended upon the bloody, rugged cross. John was one of the first disciples to run to the empty tomb of Jesus the morning of His victorious and glorious resurrection. To the arresting voice of his Lord Jesus, John attentively listened as He spoke His final words of commands and instructions to the disciples. John's eyes inquisitively gazed upon his Lord as the feet of Jesus began to lift off the Mount of Olives and He ascended into the clouds from their sight!

John did not see Jesus again until now! It was before this same Jesus that John now stood, in the Spirit, and received a great unveiling and a new Revelation of Jesus Christ! Jesus' countenance and appearance was not the same as when John last looked upon his Lord. As John turned to look upon the One who spoke to him, he saw the majestic Lord. Jesus stood as One with command and authority among His ministers and church. John described Jesus in His glorious splendor! John gazed upon Jesus clothed with a garment down to His feet signifying His position of Priest and Judge. Jesus had a golden girdle, or belt, about His waist suggesting His deity and representative of His dignity and majesty. The head and hair of the glorified Jesus were white as wool and snow; significant of His eternality, purity, and holiness. Jesus' eyes were like flames of fire which speaks of His penetrating scrutiny into the hidden motives of one's works. In righteousness, He will enact divine judgment upon all that is impure and all works will be tried as by fire, 1 Corinthians 3:13. The feet of fine brass are symbolic of His divine judgment upon sin and His enemies. The voice of Jesus resonated with resistless majesty! His was the voice of authority described in Psalm 29. When the Creator speaks, creation listens and obeys! Years before, when John walked with Jesus during His earthly ministry he embraced his Lord. In the presence of the majestic, glorified King of Heaven, John fell down as dead! What a difference in Jesus' appearance and John's approach! This eliminates the mystery of how one will react when one appears before the Lord Jesus. Yet, the Lord Jesus spoke words of comfort to John, as He will to all His children, when He touched John and said, "Fear not:" (Revelation 1:17).

Interestingly, there are thirty-four references in the twenty-two chapters of Revelation of Jesus Christ as the Lamb. The next glimpse of the Lord Jesus in Heaven will be as the "Lamb that was slain" as seen in Revelation, Chapters 4-5. Jesus Christ as the Lamb is the central figure in Revelation. Dr. Walvoord shares an excerpt from H. H. Snell's work on *Notes on the Revelation*:

> In the Revelation, THE LAMB is the centre around which all else is clustered, the foundation on which everything lasting is built, the nail on which all hangs, the object to which all points, and the spring from which all blessing proceeds. THE LAMB is the light, the glory, the life, the Lord of heaven and earth, from whose face all defilement must flee away, and in whose presence fulness of joy is known. Hence, we cannot go far in the study of the Revelation, without seeing THE LAMB, like direction-posts along the road, to remind us that He who did by Himself purge our sins is now highly exalted, and that to Him every knee must bow, and every tongue confess.[66]

Throughout the journey of the Book of Revelation, the Lamb will be presented in a different manner than in the previous chapters. No longer will Jesus Christ, the 'Lamb of God', be the meek, humble servant as a lamb being led to the slaughter, but He will be the 'Lamb' worthy of worship, alive forevermore, the One who has all authority in Heaven and earth, and the Overseer of the future prophetic events in heaven and on earth.

In obedience to the command of Christ in Revelation 4:1, "Come up hither", John was transported (raptured) into the very portals of Heaven. As a representative of the true Church of Christ, John was to view the future events from a heavenly perspective. Immediately, John was before the throne of God! Unable to make out the likeness of the

---

[66] John F. Walvoord, *The Revelation Of Jesus Christ* (Chicago, Illinois: Moody Press, 1966), 27.

One who sat upon the throne, John described His appearance in the vibrant colors of jasper, sardine, and emerald stones, Revelation 4:3. There is no doubt that John stood before the throne of God. McGee suggests this is the throne of the Triune God.[67]

John witnessed heavenly seraphim before the throne ceaselessly worshipping, calling out, "Holy, holy, holy, Lord God Almighty, which was, and is, and is to come" (Revelation 4:8b). Simultaneously, twenty-four elders representing the true church fell down before the throne and cast their God given crowns at the feet of Him who sat upon the throne. They reverently acknowledge God's worthiness of worship because He is the Almighty God and the Creator of all things, Revelation 4:10-11. It is Christ Jesus who can be seen here, for the Scriptures identify Jesus as the One who created all things. One reads in Colossians 1:16-17, "For by him were all things created, that are in heaven, and that are in earth, visible and invisible, whether they be thrones, or dominions, or principalities, or powers: all things were created by him, and for him." *Jesus Christ, the Lamb, is worthy of worship as the Creator*! He is worthy to receive glory, and honor, and power!

In the fifth chapter of Revelation, John continues to witness the events unfolding in Heaven and his focus turns toward a book within the right hand of Triune God, who sat upon the throne. The mysterious book, or scroll, was written on both the front and back and was sealed with seven seals. This book was very significant and important. So much so, that there seemed to be no one who was worthy to take the book from the hand of God. A "strong" (powerful) angel proclaimed throughout Heaven, "Who is worthy to open the book, and loose the seals thereof?" It seems all activity in Heaven ceased as a search ensued for one worthy to take the book. John's heart broke as it seemed no one worthy could be found. "And I wept much, because no man was found worthy to open and to read the book, neither to look thereon" (Revelation 5:4). Thankfully, however, one of the elders consoled John and announced there was One that was competent to take the book

---

[67] J. Vernon McGee, *Thru The Bible, Volume V* (Nashville, Tennessee: Thomas Nelson publishers, 1983), 930.

and identified Him as "the Lion of the tribe of Judah and the Root of David". Both titles refer to prophetic passages concerning Jesus. In Genesis 49:9-10, He is the Lion of Judah and Jesus is the Root, or offspring, of King David, in Isaiah 11:1, 10. Walvoord writes that in the Book of Revelation, " … Christ is referred to as the Lion only once, here in 5:5, in contrast to the many times He is identified as the Lamb. The purpose of the use of the term "lamb" seems to be to identify the glorified Christ of Revelation with Christ the Lamb of sacrifice in His first coming."[68] Chapter five of Revelation reveals Jesus Christ as the Lamb—the Redeemer! What was contained in the book that required Someone so uniquely special to retrieve it from God?

There remains much speculation and various conclusions among scholars as to the identity of this book. This writer submits this is the book of redemption and it contains the title deed to creation. One needs to turn to the Old Testament for understanding of this truth. Within the Pentateuch, the first five books of the Bible, there is recorded the Jewish law of redemption. This law dealt with the redemption of three things: a slave, a wife, and land (or a possession). In Leviticus 25:35-55, one finds the law of redemption concerning one sold into slavery. If a man became indebted to another, due to his own negligence or misfortune, and was found by law unable to satisfy the debt, the man would become a servant to the lender until the debt was satisfied. There were three exceptions to this: 1) the law provided that after he served six years, the man could be freed from his debt; 2) at anytime during the six years, the slave could redeem himself by meeting the terms of redemption and satisfying the debt; this was very unlikely to happen since he was now a slave and not working for wages; 3) at anytime within the six years, a close relative, a near kinsman, could meet the terms of redemption and satisfy the debt for his kinsman and he would be set free. "After that he is sold he may be redeemed again; one of his brethren may redeem him: Either his uncle, or his uncle's son, may redeem him, or any that is nigh of kin unto him of his family may redeem him; or if be able, he may redeem himself" (Leviticus 25:48-49).

---

[68] John F. Walvoord, *The Revelation Of Jesus Christ*, 115.

In the case of a wife, Deuteronomy 25:5-10, a law is provided whereby if a man die leaving his wife childless, the dead man's brother was to take the widow for his wife and perpetuate the name of his deceased brother. "If brethren dwell together, and one of them die, and have no child, the wife of the dead shall not marry without unto a stranger: her husband's brother shall go in unto her, and take her to him to wife, and perform the duty of an husband's brother unto her" (Deuteronomy 25:5).

Provision was made for redemption of land in Leviticus 25:23-25. According to M. R. De Haan, if a man became so indebted that he lost his property, he would be taken before a judge and a document was prepared which included: the title of the land had been transferred from the debtor to the one to whom the debt was owed; it would include the terms of redemption which would need to be meet before the property could be returned to the original owner. The terms of redemption for the title deed would be written on both sides of a scroll. The inside of the scroll contained the secret record and the outside contained the terms of redemption for public information, especially for any kinsman who might choose to redeem this possession. This scroll would be rolled up and placed into a tube and sealed with seven seals and stored in the Temple.[69]

Jesus Christ is the Kinsman Redeemer! He took upon Himself the flesh and became Man. He came unto His own. It was through His death and shed blood He met the terms of redemption for those sold into the slavery of sin by Adam. The price for man's redemption was death. God demonstrated His love for us, in that while we were still sinners, Jesus Christ died for us, Romans 5:8. It is by Jesus Christ, "In whom we have redemption through his blood, the forgiveness of sins, according to the riches of his grace" (Ephesians 1:7).

Through His death and shed blood, Jesus Christ redeemed His bride, the Church! In Ephesians 5:25-27 one reads, "Husbands love your wives, even as Christ also loved the church, and gave himself for

---

[69] M. R. De Haan, *Revelation* (Grand Rapids, Michigan: Zondervan Publishing, 1946, Thirty-second printing, 1982), 90-91.

it; That he might sanctify and cleanse it with the washing of water by the word, That he might present it to himself a glorious church, not having spot, or wrinkle, or any such thing; but that it should be holy and without blemish." The New Testament Church is identified as the Bride of Christ, or the Bride of the Lamb, in Revelation 19:7-9; 21:9.

In the scene in the fifth chapter of Revelation, one finds surrounding the throne those who have been redeemed by the blood of the Lamb and the Church which is the Bride of Christ, as represented by the twenty-four elders. The elder encouraged John not to weep, for the Lion of the tribe of Judah had prevailed to take the book from the hand of the One on the throne. John turned and saw, not a Lion, but "a Lamb as it had been slain " (Revelation 5:6). As a poignant reminder, the marks of His suffering and stripes for the redemption of man will be seen on Jesus Christ! It was Jesus Christ, the Lamb of God, who was able to take the book and break the seals, claiming ownership of the redeemed property. What property? It was creation itself!

When Adam was created he was given dominion over all the earth. Upon his sin and disobedience, he sold himself to slavery to sin. Dominion of the earth was transferred to Satan, the deceiver. Because of Adam's sin, the entire earth and creation fell under the curse. Thorns and weeds began to grow, work became hard and difficult, creation began to deteriorate, man began to age, and death was experienced for the first time. Scripture reveals, "For we know that the whole creation groaneth and travaileth in pain together until now" (Romans 8:22). "The Lord Jesus Christ is the only One who has the right and title to this earth. He not only redeemed you and me, but He also redeemed the earth."[70] The book found in the heavenly Temple of God was the title deed to creation.

Jesus Christ, the Lamb, is worthy of worship as the Redeemer! Spontaneous worship ensued when the Lamb took the book! The four beasts, the twenty-four elders and the raptured redeemed (the Church) in heaven fell before the Lamb and in unison began to sing the song of the redeemed! "Thou art worthy to take the book, and to open the

---

[70] J. Vernon McGee, *Thru The Bible, Volume V.*, 935.

seals thereof: for thou wast slain, and hast redeemed us to God by thy blood out of every kindred, and tongue, and people, and nation" (Revelation 5:9). Then innumerable angelic voices of heaven joined the worship of the Lamb, "Saying with a loud voice, Worthy is the Lamb that was slain to receive power, and riches, and wisdom, and strength, and honour, and glory, and blessing" (Revelation 5:12). In one accord, every creature in heaven, on earth, under the earth, and in the sea join voices to worship and praise God and the Lamb! The Lord Jesus not only created us and all things, but He redeemed (purchased) all things unto Himself. He owns us twice!

It is *Jesus Christ, the Lamb, who is worthy to open the seals*, reveal, and direct the judgments which are soon to fall upon the earth. The wrath of the Lamb, or the wrath of God, is mentioned thirteen times in Revelation. Now, the wrath of the Lamb is about to be unleashed upon the unrighteous inhabitants of the earth, Revelation 6:11-16. Fear will grip the inhabitants of the earth as they seek to hide from the wrath of the Lamb. The Lamb declared in Scripture who came to earth in love and grace now stands before the same earth in righteous wrath. "For the great day of his wrath is come; and who shall be able to stand?" (Revelation 6:17). Jesus Christ, the Lamb, is about to move from intercessor of the church, (the church is now with Him), and become Judge. The Redeemer is about to purge His creation from all that defiles! For the next seven years on earth, the inhabitants experience severe tribulation of multiple judgments and plagues. However, even now the Righteous Judge answers the prayer of the prophet Habakkuk, "in wrath remember mercy" (Habakkuk 3:2c). The Lord continues to extend the offer of salvation to all who would repent and trust the Lamb of God as Savior. In Revelation 7:9-17, Scripture reveals that a multitude of people do repent of their sin and are saved, but must seal their testimony by their death. "These are they which came out of the great tribulation, and have washed their robes, and made them white in the blood of the Lamb." This multitude of tribulation saints is joined with the angels and together they *worship the Lord Jesus Christ, the Lamb, for saving them from the eternal wrath to come.* Worthy is the Lamb!

The aforementioned individuals (tribulation saints), who during the seven years of tribulation on earth, repented of their sin and confess Jesus Christ as their Savior and Lord overcame tremendous obstacles and conflicts through the power of the Lamb of God. Scripture reveals they defeated Satan "by the blood of the Lamb, and by the word of their testimony; and they loved not their lives unto the death" (Revelation 12:11). These tribulation saints united in singing the song of Moses (the song of deliverance from oppression), and the song of the Lamb (the song of redemption), Revelation 15:3. Worthy is the Lamb!

In Revelation 19:1-10, Scripture unveils the heavenly marriage of the Lamb. The Bride of Christ, the Church, will present herself to Jesus Christ. She will be arrayed in fine linen, symbolic of true and pure righteousness. All of Heaven will join in the celebration and wedding festivities of singing, praises, and a marriage supper. "Blessed are they which are called unto the marriage supper of the Lamb" (Revelation 19:9a). *Jesus Christ is worthy of worship as the Heavenly Bridegroom*, for He purchased His Bride with His own blood!

The seven years of great tribulation on earth will conclude with the second coming of the Lord Jesus Christ. At this time, Christ will establish Himself upon the throne of David as "KING OF KINGS AND LORD OF LORDS" and reign upon the earth for a millennium. Christ's rule will commence with the exile of the beast and false prophet into the eternal lake of fire and brimstone. The Lord Jesus will have Satan bound and cast into the bottomless pit for the entirety of the one thousand years, Revelation 19:11-20:6. True peace will finally reign on earth! *Jesus Christ is worthy of worship as the King of Kings!*

Certainly, the saddest passage contained in the entire Bible is the great white throne judgment found in Revelation 20:11-15. God's throne of grace is about to become a throne of judgment! This judgment will include all who rejected God's offer of salvation through the blood of the Lamb of God, Jesus Christ. Everyone will stand before the throne of God without excuse, for they will be standing before the One they refused as Savior and Lord. Herein, the Scriptures of John 3:17-19 come to fruition. Jesus said, "For God sent not his Son into the world to condemn the world; but that the world through him might be saved.

He that believeth on him is not condemned: but he that believeth not is condemned already, because he hath not believed in the name of the only begotten Son of God. And this is the condemnation, that light is come into the world, and men loved darkness rather than light, because their deeds were evil." Sadly, all who stand at this judgment will be condemned to spend eternity in hell. "And death and hell were cast into the lake of fire. This is the second death. And whosoever was not found written in the book of life was cast into the lake of fire" (Revelation 20:14-15). Throughout eternity these condemned souls will be reminded they could have been spared this suffering through Jesus Christ. Their suffering will continue throughout eternity without any mercy and they will be tormented in the presence of the holy angels and in the presence of the Lamb, Revelation 14:10. *Jesus Christ, the Lamb, is worthy of worship as the Judge before whom all will bow and confess Him as LORD!*

In John 14:1-3, Jesus Christ informed His disciples that He was going away to prepare a place for His followers where they would spend eternity with Him. This promise finds fulfillment in the twenty-first and twenty-second chapters of Revelation. Within these chapters, one finds the Lord providing a new heaven, a new earth, and a new Jerusalem. The Lamb has a significant role and prominent position, for He is mentioned seven times within these two chapters. Contained in the glorious description of this magnificent eternal dwelling place is the fact that the Lamb will be the central figure. The Lamb will be the temple, and the light. Those present will be there because their names have been found written in the Lamb's Book of Life. The eternal home of the saints will inhabit the throne of God and the Lamb. A pure river of life will flow out of the throne. In this prepared place, there will be no night, no curse, no death, no sickness, no pain, no suffering, no sin, and nothing that defiles! Jesus restores the Paradise lost by Adam into a beautiful celestial city, Heaven! However, as wonderful as that will be, the most glorious and exciting event will be—the saints shall see and behold the beautiful face of their Savior! Faith will have become sight! Oh, what a day that will be, hallelujah! *Jesus Christ, the Lamb, is worthy of worship as the Faithful and True—the Promiser!*

At this point in the journey, join your hearts and voices in praise to the Lamb of God who is worthy of our praise. There is a popular song which beautifully presents our praise and worship:

Worthy is the,
Lamb who was slain
Holy, holy is He
Sing a new song, to Him who sits on
Heaven's mercy seat ...
Jesus, Your Name is Power
Breath, and Living Water
Such a marvelous mystery.[71]

In conclusion, WORTHY IS THE LAMB:

1) Jesus Christ, the Lamb, is worthy of worship as the Creator!

2) Jesus Christ, the Lamb, is worthy of worship as the Redeemer!

3) Jesus Christ, the Lamb, is worthy to open the seals of judgment!

4) Jesus Christ, the Lamb, is worthy of worship for remembering mercy in the time of wrath!

5) Jesus Christ, the Lamb, is worthy of worship for extending His salvation to those going through the tribulation on earth!

6) Jesus Christ, the Lamb, is the worthy of worship as the Groom for the Bride of Christ!

7) Jesus Christ, the Lamb, is worthy of worship as the KING OF KINGS AND LORD OF LORDS!

---

[71] Phillips, Craig, and Dean, *Revelation Song* (AZLyrics, 2000-2014), http://www.azlyrics.com/phillipscraigdean/revelationsong.html, accessed August 6,2014 at 8:38 AM.

8) Jesus Christ, the Lamb, is worthy of worship as the Judge before whom all will bow and confess Him as LORD!

9) Jesus Christ, the Lamb, is worthy of worship as the Faithful and True—the Promiser!

Jesus Christ is worthy of our devotion and surrender. "And the Spirit and the bride say, Come. And let him that heareth say, Come. And let whosoever will, let him take the water of life freely" (Revelation 22:17).

BEHOLD THE LAMB OF GOD! WORTHY IS THE LAMB! JESUS!

CONCLUSION

What is the root of the problems of the world today? Sin! What did Jesus Christ come to atone for and take away? Sin! Therefore, the answer to today's problems is Jesus Christ! Why then does mankind not turn to, and trust in, Jesus Christ? They are blinded from the truth by the false teachings promoted by the father of lies—Satan! However, the problem does not rest upon the false teachers and preachers of a false gospel. There have always been false teachers and promoters of a counterfeit gospel. The problem rests on the true church that has become silent in proclaiming the truth of salvation in Jesus Christ. The difference in the church described in the Book of Acts and the church of today is the church in Acts shared the gospel of Jesus Christ as the answer to the problems of the day and the church of today is being silenced.

Everything God has to offer man and desires to do for man is centered around what man does with His Son, Jesus Christ. Salvation, forgiveness, peace, love, heaven, etc., is wrapped up in Jesus and becomes ours through faith in Christ! "Blessed be the God and Father of our Lord Jesus Christ, who hath blessed us with all spiritual blessings in heavenly places in Christ:" (Ephesians 1:3). Herein lies the devil's purpose of his false teachers—to confound the simplicity of the gospel of Christ, 2 Corinthians 11:3. 'Jesus is the answer' is not simply a cliché—it is a great truth!

The crimson flow of the sacrificial blood of Jesus Christ is the heart of the entire Bible. This theme connects the Old Testament and the New Testament. Note the following observations: The Old Testament is divided into three sections: the Law, the Prophets, and the Psalms, according to Jesus in Luke 24:44.

The Law consists of the first five books of the Bible, with the Book of Leviticus being the heart of the Law. Contained within this book is the description of the various feasts, with the Day of Atonement being the heart of Leviticus, Chapters 16-17. The heart of these chapters is Leviticus 17:11, "For the life of the flesh is in the blood, and I have given it to you upon the altar to make atonement for your souls; for it is the blood that maketh an atonement for the soul." What is the Holy Spirit teaching us: "the blood of Jesus Christ his Son cleanseth us from all sin" (1 John 1:7b).

The heart of the second section, the Prophets, is the Book of Isaiah. Isaiah 53 is undoubtedly the heart of this great book. The heart of this chapter is found in verses 5-6, "But he was wounded for our transgressions, he was bruised for our iniquities: the chastisement of our peace was upon him; and with his stripes we are healed. All we like sheep have gone astray; we have turned every one to his own way; and the LORD hath laid on him the iniquity of us all." What is the Holy Spirit teaching us: "the blood of Jesus Christ his Son cleanseth us from all sin" (1 John 1:7b).

The heart of the third section, the Psalms, could very easily be Chapter 22. This chapter is a prophetic look at Jesus Christ as the 'Suffering Savior', with verse one being its heart. "My God, my God, why hast thou forsaken me?" is a prophetic statement of Jesus Christ on the cross centuries later. What is the Holy Spirit teaching us: "the blood of Jesus Christ his Son cleanseth us from all sin" (1 John 1:7b).

The New Testament is also divided into three sections: the Gospels, the Epistles, and Revelation. The heart of the Gospels, the first four books of the New Testament, is the Book of John. John 3 is the heart of John, with verses 14-16 being the heart of this chapter. "And as Moses lifted up the serpent in the wilderness, even so must the Son of man be lifted up; That whosoever believeth in him should not perish, but have eternal life. For God so loved the world that he gave his only begotten Son, that whosoever believeth in him should not perish, but have everlasting life." What is the Holy Spirit teaching us: "the blood of Jesus Christ his Son cleanseth us from all sin" (1 John 1:7b).

The heart of the second section, the Epistles, definitely is the Book of Romans. Within this profound theological book, one is drawn to its heart in Chapter 5 and verses 8-9. "But God commendeth his own love toward us, in that, while we were yet sinners, Christ died for us. Much more then, being now justified by his blood, we shall be saved from wrath through him." What is the Holy Spirit teaching us: "the blood of Jesus Christ his Son cleanseth us from all sin" (1 John 1:7b).

The heart of the final section, Revelation, must be Chapter 1 which describes the glorified Christ. Verses 5-6 of the first chapter of Revelation provides us the heart of this chapter, " … Unto him who loved us, and washed us from our sins in his own blood, And has made us kings and priests unto God and his Father; to Him be glory and dominion for ever and ever. Amen." What is the Holy Spirit teaching us: "the blood of Jesus Christ his Son cleanseth us from all sin" (1 John 1:7b).

Is there any wonder why Satan has attacked the message of the 'blood of Jesus Christ' as essential for our salvation? Sadly, the devil has been successful in silencing this message in many pulpits and simply replacing the message with only the love of God, or a prosperity gospel, or a bloodless gospel. Without the message of Jesus' vicarious suffering and His shed blood for our sins, one cannot begin to understand and appreciate the love of God! The power of redemption, the power to save, and the basis of forgiveness is only in the blood of Christ Jesus! "In whom we have redemption through his blood, the forgiveness of sins, according to the riches of his grace" (Ephesians 1:7).

"For he hath made him to be sin for us, who knew no sin; that we might be made the righteousness of God in him" (2 Corinthians 5:21). Jesus Christ did not simply atone, or cover, our sin; He is the 'Lamb of God' who *took away* our sin! He provided for us the acceptable covering of righteousness, *His* righteousness that allows us access to a relationship with Holy God. Jesus Christ accomplished for us what we needed, but was unable to accomplish for ourselves! He did more than provide 'fire' insurance for those who trust in Him as Savior—Jesus saved us from the wrath of God!

The vicarious suffering and the blood of Jesus Christ is the reason why, "That if you confess with thy mouth the Lord Jesus, and shalt believe in thine heart that God hath raised him from the dead, thou shalt be saved. For with the heart man believeth unto righteousness; and with the mouth confession is made unto salvation ... For whosoever calls upon the name of the Lord shall be saved" (Romans 10:9-10, 13). "How shall we escape, if we neglect so great salvation;" ... (Hebrews 2:3a). Trust in Jesus Christ today!

Thank you for embarking with me on this incredible journey down the crimson path. Together, we have unveiled the 'mystery of the gospel' by discovering and evaluating the 'foreshadows' of the 'Lamb of God' in the Old Testament which culminated in the 'fulfillment' of the 'Lamb of God' in the New Testament. Together, we have traveled from the paradise of God within the Garden of Eden to the eternal, celestial City of God promised to every believer in the 'Lamb of God'—Jesus Christ! Hopefully, you have been introduced to the unfathomable love of God, His amazing grace, His abounding mercy, and His complete and incomprehensible work of redemption for the salvation of your soul. The cleansing power is in the blood of the Lamb! Oh, what a Savior! Praises and Glory to our Lord Jesus Christ! Worthy is the Lamb!

BIBLIOGRAPHY

Allen, Jerry. *The Scarlet Cord: Foreshadows of Christ-A Mystery Revealed.* BookSurge Publishing, 2009.

Boice, James Montgomery. *Philippians: An Expositional Commentary.* Grand Rapids, Michigan: Baker Books, 1971, 2000. Paperback edition 2006.

Cabal, Ted, ed. *The Apologetics Study Bible.* Nashville, Tennessee: Holman Bible Publishers, 2007.

Chafer, Lewis Sperry. *Systematic Theology, Eight volumes published in Four.* Grand Rapids, Michigan: Kregel Publications, 1948, 1976.

Combs, James O. *Rainbows From Revelation.* Springfield, Missouri: Tribune Publishers, 1994.

Davis, John. *Paradise to Prison Studies in Genesis.* Grand Rapids, Michigan: Baker Book House, 1975.

De Haan, M. R. *Revelation.* Grand Rapids, Michigan: Zondervan Publishing, 1946, Thirty-second printing, 1982.

Edersheim, Alfred. *The Life and Times of Jesus the Messiah,* Tenth Printing-September 2009. Peabody, Maine: Hendrickson Publishers, 1993.

Edershiem, Alfred. *The Temple: Its Ministry and Services.* Peabody, Massachusetts: Hendrickson Publishers, 1994. Eight Printing, 2009.

Falwell, Jerry, ex. ed. *The Liberty Annotated Study Bible, King James Version.* Lynchburg, Virginia: Liberty University, 1988.

Fruchtenbaum, Arnold G. *The Book of Genesis.* San Antonio, Texas: Ariel Ministries, 2009.

Fruchtenbaum, Arnold G. *Messianic Christology.* San Antonio, Texas: Ariel Ministries, 1998.

Grudem, Wayne. *Systematic Theology*. Grand Rapids, Michigan: Zondervan,1994.

Guzik, David. *"Study Guide for Genesis 2."* Enduring Word. Blue Letter Bible. 7 Jul 2006. 2013. 29 Mar 2013 <http://www. blueletterbible.org/commentaries/comm_view.cfm?Author ID=2&contentID=7322&commInfo=31&topic=Genesis &ar=Gen_2_25 >

Ironside, H. A. *The Prophet Isaiah*. Neptune, New Jersey: Loizeaux Brothers, 1952, Eleventh Printing, December 1975.

Jeremiah, David. *Thirty Amazing People in the Bible, Volumes 1 and 2*. San Diego, California: Turning Point, 2012.

Johnson, Paul. *Jesus: A Biography from a Believer*. New York, New York: The Penguin Group, 2010.

Larkin, Clarence. *The Book of Revelation*. Philadelphia, Pennsylvania: Erwin W. Moyer Co., 1919.

MacArthur, John. *The MacArthur Bible Commentary*. Nashville, Tennessee: Thomas Nelson Publishers, 2005.

MacDonald, William. *Believer's Bible Commentary*. Nashville, Tennessee: Thomas Nelson Publishers, 1995.

McGee, J. Vernon. *Thru the Bible with J. Vernon McGee, Volumes 1-6*. Nashville, Tennessee: Thomas Nelson Publishers, 1981.

Moody, D. L. *Notes from My Bible and One Thousand and One Thoughts from My Library*. Grand Rapids, Michigan: Baker Book House, Reprinted August 1979.

Newell, William R. *The Book of The Revelation*. Chicago, Illinois: Grace Publications, 1935, Sixth Printing, May, 1946.

Olford, Stephen F. *The Tabernacle: Camping with God*. Grand Rapids, Michigan: Kregel Publications, 1971, 2004 Second Edition.

Phillips, John. *Exploring Genesis: An Expository Commentary*. Grand Rapids, Michigan: Kregel Publications, 2001.

Rice, John R. *In the Beginning*. Murfreesboro, Tennessee: Sword of the Lord Publishers, 1975.

Ritchie, John. *Feasts of Jehovah: Foreshadows of Christ in the Calendar of Israel*. Grand Rapids, Michigan: Kregal Publications, Reprint 1982.

Rosen, Ceil & Moishe. *Christ in the Passover.* Chicago, Illinois: Moody Publishers, 2006.

Ryrie, Charles Caldwell. *Ryrie Study Bible, King James Version.* Chicago, Illinois: Moody Publishers, 1986, 1994.

Sheffield, Bill. *The Beginnings Under Attack.* Springfield, Missouri: 21st Century Press, 2003.

Strong, James. *The New Strong's Exhaustive Concordance of the Bible.* Nashville, Tennessee: Thomas Nelson Publishers, 1990.

Swindoll, Charles R. *Moses: A Man of Selfless Dedication.* Nashville, Tennessee: W Publishing Group, a Division of Thomas Nelson, Inc., 1999.

Swindoll, Charles R. *The Greatest Life of All: Jesus.* Nashville, Tennessee: Thomas Nelson Publishers, 2008.

The Holy Bible, New King James Version. Nashville, Tennessee: Broadman & Holman Publishers, 1996.

Vine, William E. *Isaiah: Prophecies, Promises, Warnings.* Grand Rapids, Michigan: Zondervan Publishing House, Paperback Edition, 1971.

Vine, William E. *An Expository Dictionary of New Testament Words.* Old Tappan, New Jersey: Fleming H. Revel Company, 1940, Seventeenth impression, 1966.

Wallace, Roy. *Lessons From The Tabernacle.* Shreveport, Louisiana: LinWel Ministries, 2007.

Walvoord, John. *Jesus Christ Our Lord.* Chicago, Illinois: Moody Publishers, 1996.

Walvoord, John. *The Revelation Of Jesus Christ.* Chicago, Illinois: Moody Bible Institute of Chicago, 1966.

Watts, J. Wash. *A Survey of Old Testament Teaching Vol. 1 and II.* Nashville, Tennessee: Broadman Press, 1947.

Young, Edward J. *The Book of Isaiah, Vol. 1-3.* Grand Rapids, Michigan: William B. Eerdmans Publishing Company, 1965.

Young, Robert. *Analytical Concordance to the Bible.* Grand Rapids, Michigan: William B. Eerdmans Publishing Company, 1964, Reprinted 1971.

Zodhiates, Spiros. *The Hebrew-Greek Key Study Bible.* Grand Rapides, Michigan: Baker Book House, 1984.

Printed in the United States
By Bookmasters